Exotic Barn FINDS

MATT STONE

Lamborghini, Ferrari, Porsche, Aston Martin and More

CarTech®

CarTech®, Inc.
39966 Grand Avenue
North Branch, MN 55056
Phone: 651-277-1200 or 800-551-4754
Fax: 651-277-1203
www.cartechbooks.com

© 2015 by Matt Stone

All rights reserved. No part of this publication may be reproduced or utilized in any form or by any means, electronic or mechanical, including photocopying, recording, or by any information storage and retrieval system, without prior permission from the Publisher. All text, photographs, and artwork are the property of the Author unless otherwise noted or credited.

The information in this work is true and complete to the best of our knowledge. However, all information is presented without any guarantee on the part of the Author or Publisher, who also disclaim any liability incurred in connection with the use of the information and any implied warranties of merchantability or fitness for a particular purpose. Readers are responsible for taking suitable and appropriate safety measures when performing any of the operations or activities described in this work.

All trademarks, trade names, model names and numbers, and other product designations referred to herein are the property of their respective owners and are used solely for identification purposes. This work is a publication of CarTech, Inc., and has not been licensed, approved, sponsored, or endorsed by any other person or entity. The Publisher is not associated with any product, service, or vendor mentioned in this book, and does not endorse the products or services of any vendor mentioned in this book.

Edit by Bob Wilson
Design concept by Connie DeFlorin
Layout by Monica Seiberlich

ISBN 978-1-61325-202-4
Item No. CT541

Library of Congress Cataloging-in-Publication Data Available

Written, edited, and designed in the U.S.A.
Printed in China
10 9 8 7 6 5 4 3 2 1

Front Cover: *Imagine flipping open the side doors of a drafty wood barn on a farm in agricultural central California, and finding not a single Maserati Ghibli, but three of them, plus an ex-Brian Redman Lola F5000 racing car. This is chassis number 008 rolling into the California sunshine for the first time in decades.*

Front Flap: *This is a real-deal, no-questions-asked early Euro-spec Lamborghini Miura, stacked on blocks, complete but filthy. The original supercar exotic, this goes on any list of world's greatest barn finds. Its story is shared by* Chasing Classic Cars' *Wayne Carini.*

Frontispiece: *Somewhere beneath all the crud is a gleaming jewel of a Ferrari Spyder. Original five-decade-old Celeste Blue paint remains (but could certainly stand a high-quality color sand and buff job), with all original chrome and badging in place and in generally good condition.*

Title Page: *Happy guy, happy car. Leno's super-capable Big Dog Garage crew freshened up the mechanicals, cleaned up the car, and had the mystic Gullwing back on the road in short order. Still wearing its tired original paint, race numbers, and Tony Nancy leather interior, the SL likely looks a lot like it did when last raced several decades earlier. Note that Leno runs it with the rear bumper in place but without a front bumper; this is likely how it raced originally.*

Back Cover Photos

Top: *Faded non-original paint and grungy trim notwithstanding, this Ferrari Lusso 5233 GT cuts a dashing path on its original Borrani wire wheels. Fender decals were owner added somewhere along the way, and this car remained in single-family ownership from the day it was sold new in 1963 until the summer of 2014, having lived nearly its entire life in Karachi, Pakistan.*

Middle: *This is the dream of many Alfisti. A Veloce-spec Giulia Spider tucked neatly into a covered woodshed somewhere in Europe; dirty but complete and without rust, ready for sale and rescue from slumber.*

Bottom: *That's certainly no way to treat an Aston Martin! The conditions couldn't be worse for preserving a car in storage. This DB4's past, present, and future don't look good from any angle, but it's obvious that all of the important glass, light lenses, bezels, and chrome are intact.*

OVERSEAS DISTRIBUTION BY:

PGUK
63 Hatton Garden
London EC1N 8LE, England
Phone: 020 7061 1980 • Fax: 020 7242 3725
www.pguk.co.uk

Renniks Publications Ltd.
3/37-39 Green Street
Banksmeadow, NSW 2109, Australia
Phone: 2 9695 7055 • Fax: 2 9695 7355
www.renniks.com

CONTENTS

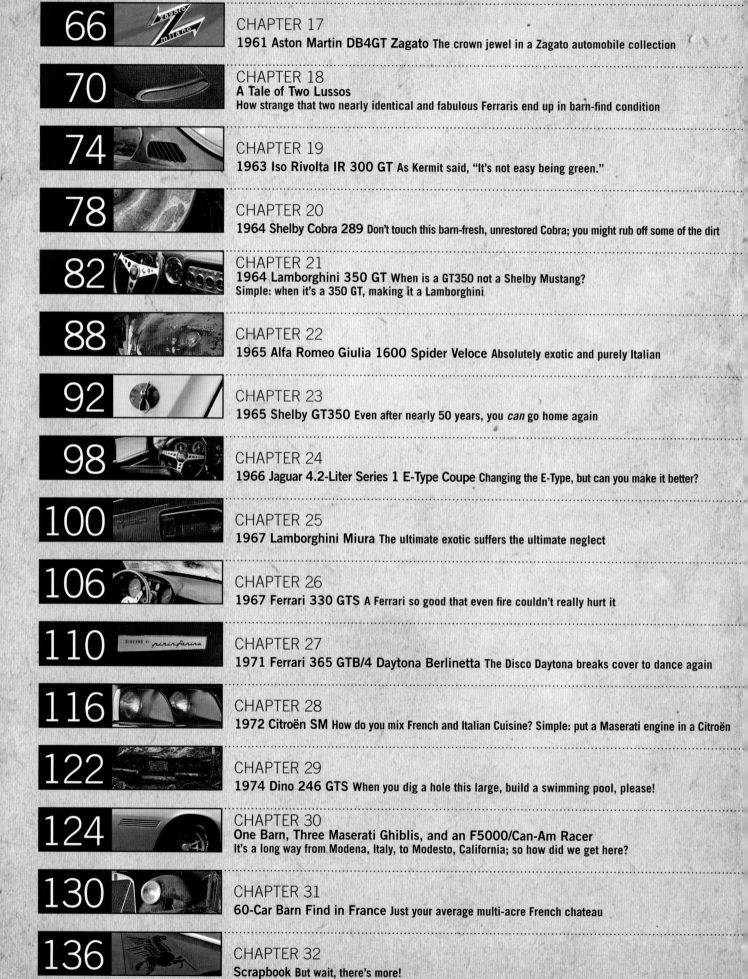

Acknowledgments

Wesley Allison, Artcurial Auctions, Beau Boeckmann, Bonhams Auctions, Chris Brown, David Brynan, Wayne Carini, Amy Christie, Corky Coker, Tom Cotter (my friend and a superb enthusiast who identified and codified the notion of modern barn find books), Galpin Auto Sports and Collection, Kirk Gerbracht, David Gooding, Gooding & Company, Jannelle Grigsby, Winston Goodfellow, Paul Hageman, Garth Hammers, Hannah Lintner, Alyssa McGovern, Leslie Kendall, Evan Klein, Jay Leno, Mullin Automotive Museum, Lynn Park, Petersen Automotive Museum, Stuart Reed, Andrew Reilly, RM Auctions, Rebecca Ruff, Tom Shaghnessy, David Sydorick, Mel Stone, Linda Stone, Mom and Dad, and everyone at CarTech Books. And all of the car owners referenced herein. Plus anyone else whose car was snapped along the way without my knowing your name.

Introduction

I've spent many hours daydreaming about why car people are so jazzed up over finding a dusty old car abandoned in a barn or garage.

Is it an update or automotive incarnation of the buried treasure fantasy? Or a spin on the notion of nostalgia? Or maybe some people automatically think they can pry that "unwanted old junker" away from a less than knowledgeable owner, sell it, and make a ton of money on the deal. Or the inner *This Old House* gene that makes us want to adopt a neglected old thing (car, dog, house, spouse, whatever) and nurse it back to health and beauty. But back to the buried treasure mentality . . . To find something valuable that nobody else knew about, dig it up, and cash in? I asked my friend Corky Coker, who owns a variety of businesses that serve the collector and classic car marketplace, and hosts a television show about barn finding cars (charmingly named *Backroad Gold*), and what he felt drove the phenom. He replied that it's a "giant mix of all those factors with a heap of human nature thrown in."

I agree.

This notion is nothing new; the hope of finding that Bugatti in a barn or the forlorn Ferrari in a field has been the fantasy of car enthusiasts for decades, but it certainly has become exponentially more popular in the last dozen or so years. Perhaps it's the growing popularity of buying and selling cars at collector and classic car auctions (often on live television), where the buyer and seller groups are larger and more diverse. The Internet certainly keeps the barn find jungle drums humming. Another likely reason is the growing appreciation for unrestored cars, originality, and the patina of use and enjoyment; although as you'll see, too many barn finds have been abused and neglected far beyond the notion of patina; many have degraded to "parts car" status, or are in genuine need of a comprehensive physical and cosmetic restoration. No matter, for many, it's the thrill of the hunt. And perhaps it's analogous to the notion of rooting around in antique shops and garage sales.

I've come to think of "barn find" as a metaphor for a car lost and found, as not every great hidden find comes directly and literally out of a barn; I hope you'll go along with me on this. But if the piece wasn't somehow lost, salted away, vanished, and then reborn into the world, it's not a barn find. Many cars have been lost; the idea here is to feature cars that have been lost (or hidden) *and found*. You'll notice that the subject here is "exotic" barn finds; please allow me a little license here as well. The idea for this volume was to include only sporty or otherwise generally "exotic" brands and models, and everyone's definition of "exotic" varies somewhat. The idea here is not to include page after page of, perhaps cool, but otherwise very average old cars. Not that I have anything against '47 Plymouths, but they're hardly exotic, so you won't find that kind of hardware herein. Yet not every exotic is a Ferrari or a Lamborghini; if you know much about automotive history and development, technology, and design, I hope you'll agree with me that many Alfas and Lancias and Isos are indeed exotic in important ways.

You would think that if someone had just uncovered a very special, rare, exotic car long stored in a barn or garage, that he or she might have brought a good camera or photographer along to capture the moment the car was exhumed, or at least the conditions under which it was parked or abandoned. But, all too often, this doesn't seem to be the case. When possible, I attempted to be present, camera in hand, when a given find was pulled out of hibernation. Because this was not always practical, I pursued the owner, dealer, or auction company for "as found" photos. When they existed, I got them and you see them here. When they didn't, the moment is all too often lost to time. Getting good quality "in situ" photos of these great finds was one of the biggest challenges of assembling this book. A couple of cars came with poor-quality cellphone photos that were just too dark, blurry, or too low in resolution to even consider publishing here. So we didn't.

I also want to call your attention to something special at the end of the book that I call the "Barn Find Scrapbook." This is a cool collection of barn-find photos for which there wasn't enough photography or story information to create a standalone chapter, but the car or what I knew of the story was too interesting to dismiss. I've put the edible leftovers into their own little scrapbook as a different way to wrap up the book. I hope you enjoy it.

And thank you for reaching into your pocket or metaphoric wallet and purchasing this book. I hope you like it.

My First Barn Find

That said, here's my very own first barn find story, even though the car itself is hardly exotic. The story is fun and absolutely true.

Most young people acquire their first car via normal channels, such as a private party or Honest John's Fine Used Cars. Or perhaps it's a hand-me-down from a parent or other relative.

Mine was dragged out of a chicken barn.

My late father was a real-estate broker in Southern California, as was I for some years. Dad had been called in to sell a mini-ranch in a rural area of Ontario, California, for a widow who was moving to the proverbial condo in Palm Springs. While surveying the property's outbuildings, he noticed a large mass, sort of resembling the shape of an automobile. It was beneath a mountain

of hay, wire fencing, lumber, at least one mattress, and multiple layers of chicken droppings. It turned out that the big pile was indeed a car. It had been parked there by the property owner's late husband and last driven many years before.

Dad's thoughts of measuring the house for the listing contract were brushed aside. He called me, and said to come quickly to help him uncover this newfound treasure: a 1954 Mercury Monterey hardtop. Sand beige, emerald-green top, two-tone interior, and lots of chrome. I was 16 at the time (awarded my driver's license at 8:30 a.m. on the day of my 16th birthday) and wanted a car (any car) more than bees want flowers. In fact, I didn't just want a car; I *needed* one. You know, to do important things, like drive myself to the local Burger Biggie to hang with my friends.

It turned out these folks were the car's original owners; they drove her off the showroom floor new in 1954. She had the latest 261-ci overhead-valve Y-block V-8, replacing the venerable flathead V-8 that had powered millions of Ford products since 1932. A little chrome badge on the trunk proclaimed that this machine was equipped with no mere transmission: It had a Merc-O-Matic! The Monterey was in original, unrestored condition, but hadn't run for a long time. And it was really dirty.

Mrs. Chicken Farmer agreed to give us the car if we cleared up the back registration and license fees, and paid the towing fee to remove it from her property. Sum total so far: $31. I had wheels! Sorta.

I'll never forget the anguished look on my mother's face when Tony's Union 76 Towing Service tooled up our middle-class, suburban street and plopped the Chicken-poopmobile in the driveway. Now, Mom was used to the "car thing." Dad had been a hot rodder since before World War II, so she'd been exposed. But this was something altogether new and embarrassing. Neighbor kids laughed. Neighbor parents called. Mom cried. And I washed.

And scrubbed. And hosed and rinsed. Underneath those layers of case-hardened dung was one gem of an automobile. Pure 1950s. Dad and I drained the gas tank, changed the spark plugs, points, condenser, rotor, engine oil, filters, and brake fluid. We cleaned and tightened and fiddled. The six-volt, tar-topped battery took two days to recharge. Would the car even run, or make any kind of noise when I finally turned the key?

As has occasionally happened with the Super Bowl, the event itself wasn't worth all the hype and worry: The Mercury fired on the first turn of the key. It was now sparkling. The whole family hopped into it and we drove the car out to dinner that night. This time, Dad and I laughed. So did Mom.

We continued to improve the Merc while preserving its original condition and patina. But there was a problem. Not with the car, but with me. Being a horsepower-hungry teen whose high-school parking lot was filled with 1960s and 1970s American muscle, the Monterey just wasn't cool enough. Dad could see, too, that while Ye Olde Merc would be good sensible transport (and goodness knows, affordable; I think our total investment thus far was about $100), I just wasn't going to be happy with it for long.

I needed something more befitting the president of the Alta Loma High School Marching Band. So I bought something a bit more appropriate, and a bit cooler: a 1971 Olds 442 with a 455-ci big-block, factory ram air fiberglass hood, and a Hurst shifter. Smack in the middle of the first gas crunch. Not so sensible. But way cool.

We sold the Merc to a neighbor, who repainted it and installed rumbling glasspack mufflers. She paid us $200, a tidy profit over our original investment. Last I knew she still had it.

Wish I did, too.

Chapter 1

1925 Bugatti Type 22 Brescia Roadster

GREAT BEAUTY LIES BENEATH

By way of disclosure, I've written about this car and its equally amazing story in another book. However, I felt that it's just so over the top interesting as a "lost and found" exotic car story it was worthy of using here to open this book. I hope you agree.

Almost any Bugatti is a special automobile for numerous reasons: Bugatti is a prestigious French marque. Many of them are spectacular examples of great automotive design and engineering. Various Bugattis were successful race cars, and one particular 1925 Bugatti Type 22 Brescia Roadster is best known for having been reputedly won in a card game, and then seized by Swiss authorities for the non-payment of duty taxes.

According to the lore and legend of the day, the French Blue sports roadster was owned by Bugatti team racing driver, and several times grand prix race winner, Rene Dreyfus, who came in contact with a Swiss national named Adalbert Bode. Bode's history is somewhat cloudy; his interests and occupations are variously noted as bartender, racing driver, and gambler. In or around 1934 in Paris, France, Bode and Dreyfus (who, after retiring from racing as a professional, owned a famous French restaurant in Manhattan, named Le Chanteclair) reportedly consumed several bottles of fine champagne and then engaged in an impromptu game of poker, with the rare Bugatti two-seater as the stakes. Dreyfus lost the game and the car.

When Bode attempted to bring his newly won prize into Switzerland, he was unable (or unwilling) to pay the duty taxes on his winnings. He reportedly left the car parked in a private garage near the small town of Ascona. Swiss law required destruction of the property in question to avoid unjust enrichment of the guilty party due to the non-payment of the taxes. The authorities, for reasons not entirely clear, chose to sink the car into Lago Maggiore, instead of merely impounding it, or perhaps

Above: *The side of the car embedded into the soft silt of the lakebed fared better than the side exposed to "clear" water. Even though the results of corrosion and theft damage are considerable, the hidden side of the car was in a sort of suspended animation; the bottom was quite dark 170 feet down, the water was fresh as opposed to salty water, and very cold.*

Facing Page: *The shape of this tidy Bugatti Roadster is now somewhat ghostly. It lives on special display at the Mullin Automotive Museum in Southern California. The car's driver's side suffered the most damage, although it's still remarkable that so much of the car remains. Unfortunately, countless divers from around the world visited the car during its decades at the bottom of Italy's Lago Maggiore. Many of them took souvenirs of their dive, such as the enameled metal Bugatti badge from the front grille.*

Below: *The car is so unique and its story so special that the Mullin Automotive Museum built a display room just for the car. It is specially lighted, attempting to replicate what the car may have looked like underwater.*

disassembling or consigning it to a dismantler. Regardless, sometime in 1934, the car was tethered to 35-foot-long steel chains and suspended off the shore in the water. The reason for the chains was that if the owner wished to pay his taxes and reclaim the car, it could, theoretically, be retrieved. To further complicate this somewhat murky situation, information also leads to another possible owner, an architect named Marco Schmuklerski who moved to Ascona at about the same time, from France.

What seemed like the proverbial "good idea at the time" proved not to be, at least from the car's perspective. Time and corrosion ultimately fatigued the chains and the hapless Bugatti broke loose and sank to the lake bottom, approximately 170 feet down. It came to rest on its passenger's side, the wheels, fenders, and some portions of the bodywork sinking into the soft silt and mud. Locals had never forgotten the story of the "The Lady in the Lake." Once it was located, it became a popular attraction for recreational divers. Among them was a young local named Damiano Tamagni.

Tamagni was attending the Carnival festival in Locarno, Switzerland, on February 1, 2008, when he

was set upon by thugs who beat him severely. The 23-year-old died as the result of his injuries from that savage attack. The motives for this murderous crime are not fully known; it may have been a robbery gone awry, but some speculate the act may have been hate-related against Tamagni for either being gay or perceived as such. Tamagni's family, along with local divers, began taking steps to rescue the Bugatti from the depths of Lago Maggiore. They planned to auction it off to benefit the charitable foundation established in Tamagni's name, the Foundazione Damiano Tamagni; its mission was to combat youth violence and hate crime.

Bringing the car to the surface of the lake proved to be a complex engineering and logistical undertaking that ultimately took nearly a year. The goal was for the Bonhams auction house to sell the car at its annual sale at the Rétromobile classic car event in Paris in early 2010. The three prime protagonists in the rescue and exhumation effort were local divers/adventurers Jens Boerlin, Nicola Sussigan, and Stefano Mattei. Despite occasional bouts of bad weather, and the sinking of a floating work platform, the team finished the job on July 12, 2009, to the cheers, tears, and applause of several thousand spectators.

Although the sporty Bug had suffered greatly from decades of submersion, a fair amount of the car remained intact; far more than if it had been in the ocean. Lago Maggiore is a freshwater lake; the corrosive effects of ocean saltwater would have been dramatically more destructive. The passenger's side of the car, which had sunk into the silty lakebed, was relatively well preserved. But the driver's side of the car, exposed to the open water and to bacteria feasting on the metal, wood, rubber, and other components of the car, suffered considerably more decay.

Damaged wheels and missing tires prevented the car from being moved easily around, so

The manufacturer's tag for the custom bodywork remains intact. All but one rivet hold it in place; otherwise the small metal tag is in excellent condition.

Bonhams' constructed a relatively simple metal dolly so the fragile chassis could be moved and transported without risking further damage. The car was also washed to remove the worst of the mud and silt impacted into the chassis and to minimize the continued corrosive effects.

Bonhams and the Foundazione were besieged with questions about the car. How and when would it be sold? What was the real story? How much was it worth? Even Bonhams' best automotive experts didn't really know the answers; selling this type of vehicle was new territory for everyone.

Restorers, collectors, and potential buyers speculated as to whether the car could, or should, be restored. Fortunately, Californians Merle and Peter Mullin along with Andrew Reilly (founders and benefactors of the Mullin Automotive Museum in Oxnard, California, and the museum's now former curator, respectively) were of the strong opinion that to restore the car would be a crime against its history.

The Mullins, a couple with considerable taste and means, are known for having one of finest collections of art deco–era French cars in the world. They have many concours-winning cars in their museum, but they felt the only proper way to respect the car's history, and pay fitting tribute to young Tamagni, was to preserve, conserve, and present the car in its as-found condition.

Bonhams consigned and auctioned the car in Paris, as planned. Peter Mullin was the winning bidder, paying $366,367 including commissions.

Curator Reilly acknowledged that his role was more of a preservationist. He needed to protect the car in its current condition and prevent further

A spare wheel remains intact, sans tire, mounted to the side of the car. Some of the car's tires survived the effects of the lake, while others must have disintegrated, leaving no trace. No amount of restoration would likely ever make it safe for road use again.

Left: *The exhaust side of the engine shows the block, head, and four-branch exhaust manifold that are largely intact. The manifold was probably porcelain coated at the factory and that helped protect it from the water's corrosive effects.*
Right: *The intake side of the engine shows the original carburetor still in place and mounted in the intake manifold. Given the number of divers that picked parts off the car, it's amazing that this piece remained.*

degradation without any actions or processes that could be deemed "restoration." The more closely Reilly inspected the car, the more of its secrets were revealed. Many of the glass-covered instruments were filled with water. The manual transmission, apparently tightly sealed when built, still held transmission oil from when the car roamed the roads and race courses of Europe.

The car is now on permanent display at the Mullin Automotive Museum, the star of its own special exhibit. It is bathed in an eerily soft and soothing light designed to mimic, to the extent possible, its appearance while submerged (although now upright, not on its side) and is surrounded by photography of the car while it lived at the bottom of Lago Maggiore.

This is what you see when you enter the Bugatti's special display area at the Mullin Museum. The effect is startling and haunting; it's also frustrating that a wonderful car was subjected to such a drastic fate. It is amazing that this much of it survives.

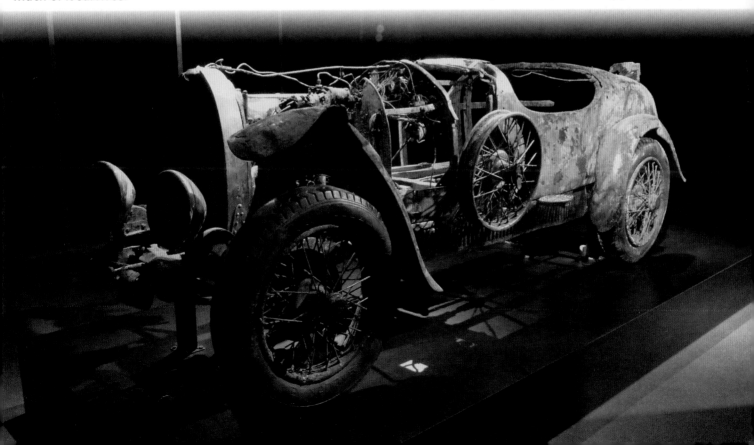

Chapter 2

The Petersen Automotive Museum's Basement Full of Muntz Jets

IF ONE IS GOOD, TWO IS BETTER, AND THREE IS BETTER STILL

The famous Petersen Automotive Museum in Los Angeles, California, is swimming in Muntz Jets. As of this writing, this important institution has three; one fully restored and another pair remaining as found in their "barn-fresh" condition.

The Muntz Jet was born out of another very similar machine, the Kurtis Sports Car (KSC). Interestingly, one of these cars is pictured on the cover of the first (September 1949) issue of *Motor Trend* magazine. Frank Kurtis was a highly successful race car constructor who built many race-winning "champ car" (Indy style) roadsters and legendary midget racers. Like many such small, independent carmakers (including Enzo Ferrari and the

Maserati brothers), Kurtis ultimately decided to design, build, and sell limited runs of street-legal sports cars to keep his employees busy when not constructing batches of racing machines, and of course to help finance race team operations.

The original KSC was a large, elegant open-topped two-seater running an American V-8 engine up front, and built on a heavy ladder-style frame with rear-wheel drive. The car, produced in Glendale, California, was expensive, and only a modest seller. Kurtis figured out that a sports car from his company needed to be smaller, lighter, and racier; it had to have a stronger connection to the racing machines he built. He therefore sold the KSC design to Earl "Madman" Muntz, at the time best known for his flamboyant, if perhaps semi-hucksterish sales and marketing of stereos and in-car entertainment systems, plus other electronic consumer and commercial goods.

Muntz had the idea to take the car even further upmarket and also felt that the demand would be stronger for a premium, open-topped four-seater instead of the original KSC's two-seat configuration. Muntz engaged future Indy 500 winning race driver Sam Hanks to help redesign and re-engineer the car into a full four-seater, riding atop an increased wheelbase chassis, with a fully *removable*, not *convertible*, Carson-style padded top. This gave the car an elegant coachbuilt look when closed, and the option of driving fully al fresco by removing the top; not exactly convenient in that there was no place to store the top in the car, so it had to be removed by at least two people then left at home. Muntz dreamed up a sumptuous all-leather tuck-and-roll interior, onboard bar (well before the days of "don't drink and drive"), and of course a Muntz in-car audio system.

Even though some of the chrome on the lettering is missing, there's no mistaking that flamboyant white convertible. Each of the Petersen Automotive Museum's newer Jets requires a complete frame-off restoration. Although one is accident damaged, they are relatively complete with lots of the extremely rare and difficult-to-replace parts present and accounted for.

The first batches of Muntz Jets were produced in Kurtis' Southern California shops but he ultimately moved the whole endeavor to Evanston, Illinois. The early cars wore aluminum coachwork and ran a Cadillac overhead-valve V-8 engine with dual carburetors. A fully equipped machine-turned metal instrument panel was stuffed full of racy Stewart Warner gauges, adding further to the Jet's appeal as an exotic sporting machine. Upon relocation in Evanston, Muntz switched to Lincoln V-8s, and the bodywork was retooled for steel panels instead of the more fragile, and more costly, aluminum alloy.

The Jets were rare and exclusive, so naturally Hollywood and entertainment types flocked to them: The movie star Grace Kelly had one, as did singing star Vic Damone and cowboy singer/actor Alfred "Lash" Larue.

Facing Page: *The Petersen has a third Jet, this one a steel-bodied Illinois-built machine that is not as prized or rare as the two aluminum-bodied barn-find cars sitting next to it. This one will also likely be sold. It will make an outstanding driver or regional show–level classic that'll be great fun to own and drive.*

Below: *The non-celebrity owned white car is in better shape than the yellow car, but its provenance is less interesting, and may be sold to help fund the other car's restoration.*

At $5,500, a Jet was about $1,500 more expensive than a top-of-the-line Cadillac convertible. Although it was heavy, the Jet was one of the fastest and best-performing American cars of the time, given its dual-carb V-8 power. Approximately 400 Muntz Jets were produced; this was about ten times the number of original KSCs built by Kurtis from 1950 to 1954. Muntz claimed that he lost money on each of the hand-built machines.

You'd expect an automotive museum with the stature of the Petersen to have a Jet in its collection, which it did. But how did one become three? Part of the museum's mission has always been to seek out, collect, and feature Hollywood cars: those either owned by entertainment celebrities or machines used in the making of television shows or movies. The museum also documents and displays the history of vehicles built in California.

The Museum already had the green Jet (shown here) in its collection when a pair of Jets found their way into the Los Angeles museum's vault. These two early, unrestored cars were of particular interest to the collection staff and curators. Curiously, both lived in long-term barn-find–style hibernation relatively close to the museum's Wilshire Boulevard location. Both wear tired, faded, chalky older paint jobs; one is pale yellow and suffered significant front-end damage early in its life while the other is off-white.

Left: *Park this next to its forebear, the Kurtis Sports Car (KSC), and it's easy to see how the extra length of about a foot made it a four-seater. Even though the Jet was never a high-volume seller, and may have actually been a money loser for Muntz, it outsold the two-seater KSC by about ten to one.* **Right:** *If one is good, then two must be fabulous. Indeed, that's the case here, as the car on the left has great celebrity provenance along with some accident damage; the car on the right is more complete and has all of the front-end grillework and sheet metal that the yellow car needs. As of this writing, the Petersen's curators have yet to finalize a restoration and display plan for these cars, but at least one of them will be fully restored while the other could be robbed of some parts and ultimately sold.*

At one time, the accident-damaged yellow Jet belonged to the famous cowboy actor, Lash Larue. Both the white and the yellow Jets are early examples produced in the Kurtis shops in nearby Glendale and are Cadillac V-8 powered with aluminum coachwork. Beyond that, the two cars are not directly connected. The Larue car was listed on eBay late in 2003 and did not sell. After that, the museum communicated with the seller and negotiated a post-auction deal to buy the car. Very shortly thereafter, the owner of the white Jet approached the museum about a potential purchase, and a deal was soon struck. All of them ended up together in the Petersen's underground storage vault. The museum was left to plan how to best manage the display and care of a trio of Muntz Jets.

At first glance, it seems logical to keep and display the green car, but it is actually of the least significance to the museum; its restoration is "driver" quality only. It has no celebrity connection and was built in Evanston, Illinois, while the other two are California Jets. Even though it has substantial front-end accident damage, the Larue car likely holds the most interest for the museum.

A number of scenarios are possible. The museum could sell the green and white cars to finance the ground-up restoration of the Larue Jet. Or it could sell the green car for the same purpose, keep the white car in unrestored barn-find condition, restore the yellow car and then display the two Jets together in a yin and yang fashion. Or the green car could be sold to finance the yellow car's restoration and the front-end sheet metal and other needed parts from the white car could be used to aid the restoration and minimize costs.

Even though the museum has ownership and possession of all three Jets, it has yet to finalize a plan. Regardless of the final decision, it appears that the green Jet will be the financing mechanism and the yellow, celebrity-owned Jet will become the show-quality prize example maintained in the museum's permanent collection.

Given that enthusiasts enjoy seeing great cars in unrestored, and, in this case, legitimate barn-find condition, I like the idea of a fully restored, gleaming, elegant Larue machine displayed alongside the as-is, barn-find white car, making for a historic and spectacular display.

A glimpse of the early Jet's aluminum bodywork is visible on this well-worn fender. The later switch to steel panels likely saved construction money and was a little easier to deal with than the more fragile and softer, but lighter alloy.

Top Left: *Another hot rod styling touch is the handmade windshield frame. It is curved at the base with a vertical split down the middle, reminiscent of the hot rodders' favorite "DuVal windshield" that graced countless customs and Deuce highboy roadsters.* **Top Right:** *A 331-ci overhead-valve Cadillac V-8 was new and hot in 1949, and thus an obvious choice for a car with as much panache as the Jet; it provided legitimate muscle car–like performance. With these dual carbs installed, it was rated at 160 hp. That doesn't sound like much now, but it was impressive in 1950.* **Bottom Left:** *The Jet cabin was plush and well appointed; occupants enjoyed lush, hand-pleated leather seating and handsome appointments.* **Bottom Right:** *The Jet's machine-turned metal instrument panel sort of resembles the Auburn and Cord dashes favored by many hot rodders and racers. In this case, it's packed full of racy Stewart Warner gauges; the four-spoke steering wheel lends a sporty touch.*

Left: *Believe it or not, this hapless-looking Jet is the pride of the litter. It's an early, California-built car with aluminum coachwork, Cadillac power, and a worthwhile Hollywood connection, but it needs a nose job and some major spa time to be beautiful again.* **Right:** *The Carson-style removable padded top is a classic custom hot rodder touch and it looks elegant in perfect condition. This one needs to be completely re-trimmed, but at least the framework and hardware are all there. This feature, while cool and attractive, might have also cost the Jet a few sales, because the top didn't fold away and could not be carried with the car. The tops on new Cadillac and Lincoln convertibles folded away easily, meaning that the decision between open and closed driving didn't have to be made at home prior to leaving for a journey.*

Chapter 3

1953 Ferrari 212 Inter Coupe by Vignale

CAT PRINTS, SPRAY PAINT, AND SPIDERWEBS. REALLY?

All photos courtesy of RM Auctions.

In spite of its forlorn looking condition in these photos, this Vignale-bodied Ferrari is a rare and special automobile. The 212 series cars were built between 1951 and 1953, in coupe and open roadster form, with models in competition and street specs.

A mere 80 were produced; some were bodied by Touring and a few by Ghia. Vignale of Turin, Italy, produced this aggressive Michelotti design. Of course, in those days, the line between race and street models tended to blur. The competizione machines were often street driven, and the somewhat milder-tuned street versions were often raced.

This car's chassis number, 0267 EU, indicates that it was intended for European delivery; the serial number ending in an odd number (7), further indicates that it was spec'd out and considered an "Inter" street model. Still formidable, the 212 series was one of the first production runs of Ferraris to make relatively high-volume use of the Colombo series single overhead cam (SOHC) V-12 engine, in this case the 2,562 cc (2.6 liters). This engine was upfitted to three Weber carburetors (like the competition models) and it produced an estimated 180 hp. The less powerful street-spec version of this engine (usually installed in this model) rated around 150. This aggressively elegant, tight, two-seat coupe is bodied in aluminum over a steel tube frame with pontoon-like fenders and headlights mounted just inboard of the front fender peaks.

Vestigial fins run along the tops of the rear fenders. The classic Ferrari egg-crate grille is a little larger and slanted more forward than on several other Ferraris of the early 1950s. The greenhouse is glassy and elegant with relatively slim pillars. Borrani wire wheels with large drum brakes are at each corner. 0267's original, understated color scheme is a black body with a light green roof. It may sound like an unusual combination, but it is extremely elegant, particularly as finished with the green interior. Several similar models were produced with this color scheme.

The 0267 was shown on Vignale's stand at the 1953 Turin Motor Show, and has been memorialized in print numerous times; it is included on page 52 of Hans Tanner's first *Ferrari Owner's Handbook*, published by Floyd Clymer in Los Angeles, but incorrectly captioned as a 250 Europa. Noted Ferrari historian Marcel Massini shows it on page 153 in his definitive book, *Ferrari by Vignale*.

Many consider the Vignale-bodied 212 the most aggressive and best looking of all 212 models. Note the aluminum-framed air intakes below the headlights. The car was originally black with a light green roof, then suffered a red paint job, prior to being repainted in the original colors. However, the beauty and gloss of that third paint job were long gone when the car was pulled out of hibernation in anticipation of its sale at auction in early 2011.

This engaging and particularly handsome Ferrari has lived a long, interesting, and international life. When new in 1953, it was initially purchased in the Southwest of France, and then driven regularly and shown at the occasional concours d'elegance. It was sold and exported to London in 1959, reputedly kept there by the same owner for a decade. In 1969, it was sold to another Englishman who kept it for only three years. The third English owner acquired the car in 1972; he removed the bumpers (perhaps for a more competition-car look) and repainted it red.

In late 1977, he sold the car to American Larry Nicklin. He is a noted car collector who owned at least two Ferraris at the time, and is one of the founding members of the Ferrari Club of America. Nicklin has also owned, built, and commissioned several notable hot rods and custom cars. In 1979, he repainted the Ferrari in its original black and green color scheme.

Left: *Lack of its original bumpers gives 0267 a competition-car look. In spite of flat paint and spray-can primer touchups, it doesn't appear to have ever been the victim of any major accident damage.* **Right:** *This Ferrari isn't really as long as the garage door behind it is wide; it's just an photographic optical illusion. Even so, the long, muscular bodylines and sleek, airy greenhouse give it the impression of being long, low, and elegant, which it certainly was for the time.*

Facing Page: *Locked away and nearly forgotten in the previous owner's garage. Sitting on nearly flat tires, the rare Ferrari 212 hadn't run in years and was clearly neglected; the long-missing bumpers are nowhere to be found, and the car has been touched up with spray-can primer along the way, perhaps with the aim of rust prevention. It's a shameful state for such a fabulous and rare automobile.*

A network of spiders must have spent years lacing their way up, down, and around this car, further evidence that it sat untouched for many years. There are certain to be a few cats' paw prints on the once-shiny black bodywork.

Although Nicklin owned this car for more than three decades, it was not seen for many years and was somewhat off the Ferrari community's radar. However, even though the car was neglected and rundown, it remained complete and in generally original condition (including its original numbers-matching 2.6-liter V-12). Many people might wonder why a Ferrari collector of such history and prominence would let a car of this stature degrade to this level. And then to sell it in such poor condition.

I asked a noted member of the Ferrari community if he knew the story. He asked to remain anonymous, but offered this well considered opinion: "None of us bought our Ferraris in the old days for any reason other than having fun with them. We never imagined that they would be worth much and drove them all the time. As time went by, the whole thing changed to a money game.

"I don't think Larry ever bought into that. He didn't use the cars much anymore, but hung on to them. Life goes by quickly. As he got older, he probably intended to get them back up to snuff, but just never got around to it.

"As we all get even older, there comes a time when you have to let things go. I'm guessing Larry had reached that point."

Nicklin consigned the car to RM Auctions for its March 2011 sale on Amelia Island, Florida, where it sold for $660,000. Until that time, it was among the highest prices paid for a "barn find" Ferrari of this model type.

Left: *At least two of the taillights are broken and are partially "repaired" with masking tape; the rear license plate must have disappeared with the bumpers. The rear metalwork appears in generally good condition.* **Right:** *Ferraris of this era that Michelotti penned and Vignale bodied are known for a big face and prominent grille; this one has both. Note the complete lack of a hood scoop and side vents, which are seen on some competizione Ferraris of the era.*

Left: *The original black leather seats appear undamaged and not consumed by mold, but the rest of the interior was likely home to numerous animals, likely very small.* **Right:** *Much to the pleasure of the owner (and restoration shop), the cabin, although filthy, is complete and original. The gauges, shifter, original steering wheel, as well as door and window handles are all present. Replacing any missing pieces would be difficult and costly.*

Left: *This engine rebuild may not be too complicated or costly because the car very likely ran when it was parked and the engine compartment is complete. However, while no Ferrari V-12 is simple or inexpensive to work on, the engines are so well known by the best Ferrari specialists that rebuilding them often presents few mysteries.* **Right:** *Many of these 212s were uprated to larger engines, including the 3.0-liter 250-series V-12. The 3.0-liter engine is an easy fit and puts out more power, but isn't original. According to RM Auctions, this is the original numbers-matching 2.6-liter V-12.* **Below:** *Out of the barn and onto a flatbed. This is often the route taken by many cars once they re-emerge from their barn slumber. Chassis number 0267 EU went to a Florida auction, on to a $660,000 sale price, and a happy new owner who has a big, yet worthwhile job ahead of him to put this historic machine back in shape and on the road.*

Chapter 4

1953 Jaguar XK120 M Fixed-Head Coupe

LIVING THE GOOD LIFE

When Jaguar first displayed its startling, sensuous XK120 in 1948, its primary purpose was as an elegant engine stand to best show off the company's new XK family of straight-6-cylinder engines. The curvaceous, feline-inspired roadster so captured the fancy of the media and public at its London Motor Show debut that Jaguar patron (later Sir) William Lyons had little choice but to immediately green-light it for production. At the time there was no closed or coupe version, just a lithe, sinewy aluminum-body open two-seater (OTS).

That original XK120 roadster wasn't in production for very long when the company began to expand its appeal by fleshing out the model lineup. That meant another open model, called the drop-head coupe or DHC, similar to the roadster but with slightly different coachwork around the rear deck area, roll-up windows, a more luxurious interior, and a built-in rather than removable folding convertible top.

The next most obvious body style to design and produce was an ultra-sophisticated closed car that came along in 1951 and was called the fixed-head coupe (FHC). Still strictly a two-seater, the FHC boasted an elegant profile in closed form, earning it the nickname "baby Bugatti." This makes sense because, particularly in profile, the new XK120 FHC did sort of resemble certain Bugatti coupes of the 1930s.

Jaguar offered, as did most carmakers, higher-performance models along the way; in the XK lineup, they were called SE (Special Equipment) or M cars. In the case of the XK120, the M-spec machine meant sportier trimming and, primarily, more horsepower. In this case, the 3.4-liter dual overhead cam straight-6 was rated at 180 hp, 20 more horses than the stock XK power output.

The XK coupe proved to be an important and popular member of the XK120 lineup, with about 2,500 closed versions sold from its debut in 1951 through 1954, the XK120's final year. The coupe body continued as the XK120, was developed into the XK140, and finally became the XK150, which wound out of production at the end of the 1960 model year, when the all-new E-Type came to market for 1961.

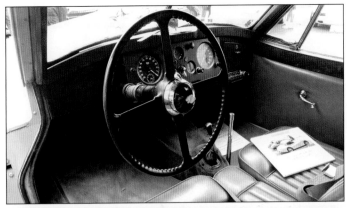

Left: *It is in the side view that the XK120 FHC most clearly earns its "baby Bugatti" nickname, particularly in the voluptuousness of the fenderlines and in the shapes of the roof and windows. Designers Sayer and Lyons clearly had French curve templates on their drawing boards when they designed this classic look.* **Right:** *The interior also glows with a warm, honest patina. The car was sold with a collection of books, manuals, and records, further evidence of its singular ownership and care.*

XK120 FHC chassis S681124 is a factory-documented M-spec model, an example of a barn find done right. It remained in single-family ownership for 58 years, and still wears its mildly patinated, entirely original pastel green paint. It was driven and enjoyed on the road for many years, then stored properly, with an obvious eye toward its preservation. It was pulled from its more than three-decade-long hibernation in 2013 and sold by the family into new ownership. It was then delivered to a noted San Francisco Bay area shop that thoroughly recommissioned it mechanically without resorting to any measurable or cosmetic restoration work. The idea was to keep it looking completely original, warts, wear, and all, while making it roadworthy and mechanically sound.

The effect is stunning and charming to behold. The soothing, original light green paint is worn in several places, mostly from years of careful washing and polishing. The original green leather interior is still relatively supple and shows no major cracks or tears; even the carpeting isn't worn through. The factory walnut trim still shines and is uncracked, showing no visible warping. The car sits on its original knock-off wire wheels, and still wears its original early-1950s California black and gold license plates.

The second owner obviously purchased the car with its recommission and resale in mind, as it was consigned with

California's Gooding & Company, to be sold at its official Pebble Beach Concours auction sale in August 2014. The seller and Gooding wisely displayed the car in clean but otherwise complete and unrestored condition, allowing its originality and history to remain completely intact.

The Gooding experts estimated the car would bring just upwards of $100,000, which proved to be close to the actual result. After enthusiastic and lively bidding, this green "baby Bugatti" was sold for $99,000 including all commissions and buyer fees. I've since heard that the happy new owner intends to drive it and show it exactly as is, and has no plans of wiping away its stories and originality with any sort of full restoration, which I heartily applaud. It's perfect just the way it is, and again to my eyes, an equally perfect example of a barn find done right.

Original, and period perfect, the California "wide black and gold" license plates look just right on a mid-1950s sports car. Note the trick add-ons for the mounting of current registration tags and stickers.

Facing Page: *From the front, there's no mistaking this car for anything but an XK120; its front sheet metal and visage are nearly identical to the iconic roadster body style first seen when the car was introduced in 1948. Here the car sits under a white translucent tent that bathes the original green body and paintwork in a lovely soothing glow. Yes, there's wear, and a few spots have been polished through to metal or primer, but the car is so faithful, its beauty shines through unfettered.*

Chapter 5

1954 Jaguar XK120SE Drop-Head Coupe

GOT DIRT?

All photos courtesy of Auctions America.

The XK120 is the car that put Jaguar on the post–World War II map as a significant maker of sports cars. The original 120 was a concept car designed to showcase the company's new "XK" dual overhead cam straight-6 engine, and the car was judged to be such a sensational design, there was no way the company couldn't put the sensuously bodied roadster into series production. It wasn't initially intended to be a race car, but they were raced with great success and set many top speed run records around the world. The XK engine, and thus the XK120, formed the DNA for the Jaguar C-Type and D-Type race cars that proved to be so successful in the 24 Hours of Le Mans in the mid-1950s.

Over time, the XK120 was offered in three similar yet somewhat distinct body styles: roadster, closed coupe, and drop-head coupe (DHC). The DHC's convertible top structure was much more integrated into its body and construction than the roadster, which had a removable and somewhat vestigial top and side curtains for windows; the DHC also had roll-up windows and a more luxuriously trimmed interior. The DHC is easy to spot; it wears slightly different door skins than the roadster, and has an extra metal plate just aft of the door opening where the side of the convertible top meets the rear fender.

The SE in this car's model designation stands for Special Equipment, which in this case means a slightly higher state of engine tune, steel wheels with chromed hubcaps (instead of the sporty, if perhaps less sturdy wire spoke wheels), stiffer suspension tuning, and dual exhaust pipes.

This somewhat forlorn example was offered for sale by Auctions America at its Spring sale in Auburn, Indiana, in May 2014. Very little was disclosed about the car's ownership or history, other than to say it was stored in a barn in the state of Georgia for some time, and was presented in its original color scheme of Jaguar Red over a dark brown leather and walnut interior; it had traveled just 60,000 miles during its 60-year life.

As you can see, the car is original somewhat to a fault, including plenty of Georgia clay and rust, both surface and structural. It still carries its original 3.4-liter XK straight-6 engine, rated at 180 hp as well as a 4-speed manual transmission.

Haggard as it may look, this former stunner was at least a runner. The consignor made the effort and investment to get the car running, primarily to demonstrate that it would and did. Auctions America presented the car in its dirty, as-found condition, which is a common practice for the marketing and sale of barn-find cars. Fortunately, the Jag was very complete at the time of sale, with no major components missing.

Speculators among the automotive community, as well as prospective bidders who surveyed the car prior to sale, wondered if it would be best bought, cleaned, fully

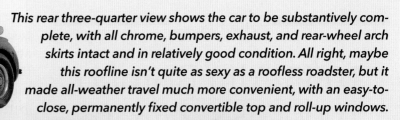

This rear three-quarter view shows the car to be substantively complete, with all chrome, bumpers, exhaust, and rear-wheel arch skirts intact and in relatively good condition. All right, maybe this roofline isn't quite as sexy as a roofless roadster, but it made all-weather travel much more convenient, with an easy-to-close, permanently fixed convertible top and roll-up windows.

Left: The original fine leather, wool rugs, and gleaming walnut had all suffered the abuse of time and barn storage, rendering the cabin virtually unusable. It certainly increased the restoration bill by several thousand dollars. **Middle:** The original dash and steering wheel were complete, which will certainly save the restorer some hassle and parts searching. **Right:** This fabulous Jaguar XK straight-6 is in somewhat faded glory. This version displaced 3.4-liter, and in SE tune, put out 180 hp; that's 20 more horsepower than in a standard XK120.

serviced, and then driven around in "shabby chic" condition, or would it be next in line for a full-scale frame-off concours-quality restoration. There's little doubt that the former plan would certainly get its driver noticed. However, most onlookers opined that the only way this car would ever be truly beautiful again was to take it down to pieces, and restore it from the ground up. Its rust needed attention, the interior was in need of the full spa treatment, the formerly gleaming walnut trim was too dusty and dull to appreciate, and the seats and carpeting were too dirty and moisture damaged to be considered elegant or luxurious.

The car was offered for auction with no reserve, meaning it would simply sell to the highest bidder, which on May 10, 2014, turned out to be $45,100 including all auction fees and premiums. The car received a very enthusiastic reception from the assembled crowd when it rolled onto the auction block under its own power,

and some people felt that the price was a bargain. Others felt it was too much given the amount of work and expense necessary to redo the car.

The buyer either felt he got such a great bargain that there was profit to be made on the resale of the car, or he realized he'd bitten off more than he could chew given the extensive (and expensive) nature of a full high-quality restoration, because the car was resold at another auction just a few months later, for nearly the same price.

This model's interior design is unusual in that the instrument panel is in the center of dashboard to be viewed equally by driver and passenger. No vinyl faux wood trim here; just genuine polished walnut. The odometer shows approximately 60,000 original miles.

Facing Page: The state of Georgia is a lovely and historic part of the world, but its often moist, claylike soil doesn't appear to have been too kind to this somewhat rare Special Equipment Jaguar drop-head coupe (DHC). Less than optimal protection from the elements, and the likelihood of long-term storage on a damp dirt floor, certainly took their toll on the car's top, interior, and bodywork.

Chapter 6

1955 Alfa Romeo 1900C SS Zagato Coupe

LIVED A LONG, HARD LIFE, AND READY FOR ANOTHER

This elegant, if rumpled looking, Zagato-bodied Alfa 1900 has an interesting development history, plus this particular car, chassis 1947, has a unique specific history. Auction house Gooding & Company shared its history in preparation for its annual Pebble Beach sale in August 2014:

"Brilliantly engineered by Orazio Satta Puliga, Alfa Romeo's 1900 series debuted to great acclaim at the 1950 Paris Motor Show and quickly achieved commercial success.

"As Alfa Romeo's first model built on a standardized production line with unitized construction and available left-hand drive, the 1900 swiftly evolved into the short-wheelbase 1900C (with C denoting "corto" or short) and the more-powerful 1900TI Super, also known as the 1900SS or SuperSprint, with enlarged 1,975-cc engines. The ultra-rare C SS combined the short chassis with a racing specification engine, gearbox, and revised final drive ratios, plus air-cooled Alfin self-adjusting brakes.

"The excellent 5-speed manual gearbox featured synchronized second, third, and fourth gears, with carefully selected ratios matching the power curve of the twin-cam Tipo 1308 engine.

"This car is equipped with a Tipo 1306 engine and is accompanied by two additional Tipo 1306 spare engines, but does not feature a correct Tipo 1308 engine. The 1900 series basked in competition success and, particularly, the success of the 1900SS with the 1900's racing credentials earned at the major races and rallies of the era, including the Targa Florio, Stella Alpina, and Mille Miglia.

"July 1959 marked the end of nearly a decade of 1900 production. Although more than 21,000 1900-series cars were built (along many variations), only 854 were the ultimate-specification 1900C SS. From introduction, the 1900 received the deft touch of Italy's finest custom coachbuilders, including Touring, Ghia, Vignale, and

Above: *It is not one of Zagato's compelling "double bubble" designs, but it is handsome nonetheless. The stance is purposeful, and this shape could have easily been built on a Ferrari chassis in the mid-1950s.*

Facing Page: *Zagato drew this amazing Alfa's alloy body design tightly onto the 1900-series' short sport chassis. The Alfa nose and grille are prominent and brand identifying, and the rest of the design gets by with minimal adornment and superb proportions. This car still shows the timeworn, mismatched finish of its original silver.*

Zagato, which used ultra-lightweight alloy panelwork, yielded even greater performance.

"Finished in gray and delivered on May 13, 1955, this Zagato-bodied Alfa Romeo 1900 CSS, chassis AR1900C*01947 was sold through the Alfa Romeo dealership in Lucca, Tuscany, to Luigi DePaoli, who was known to have owned a succession of fascinating cars. The vehicle was returned to Alfa Romeo soon thereafter, and Charlie Daniels, a member of the U.S. military in Italy, and Colonel William Kelly acquired it. The men campaigned the car jointly until 1957, when Colonel Kelly took sole ownership of the car.

Left: *Gooding & Company properly disclosed that the original engine was not installed, noting: "This car is equipped with a Tipo 1306 engine and is accompanied by two additional Tipo 1306 spare engines, and does not feature a correct Tipo 1308 engine."* **Right:** *Given the amount of time this car spent on the racetrack, it's no surprise that its corners have suffered a bit. Note that the original bumperettes are missing, and that most of the paint touchups were done with a brush.*

The beautiful cloisonné badge of the Scuderia Aurelia car club cleverly incorporates the shape of Italy in its graphics and logo. If this were missing, replicating it or finding a replacement would be difficult, if not impossible.

"Colonel Kelly served 28 years in the army, eventually rising to the rank of brigadier general. While traveling through Europe, he entered club tours and rallies with 01947, the majority of which were likely organized by the Scuderia Aurelia (not associated with the Lancia model of the same name) club at Camp Darby.

"The cloisonné badge of this exclusive club is still affixed to the front of the 1900's thin aluminum bonnet. Following Brigadier General Kelly's return to the United States and a new posting in North Carolina, the SSZ was stored unused in relative secrecy from 1977. The Alfa Romeo was retained by Brigadier General Kelly for nearly 60 years in all, until its recent discovery and acquisition by the consignor.

"Racing is generally a tough life for a car, and this elegant Alfa displays its battle scars proudly. The thin piece of chromed tubing affixed to the car's front bumper brackets is, of course, not the original bumper. The car wears exceptionally tired silver paint, some of which is likely original, although certainly not that of the driver's door, which mismatches the rest of the car by considerable difference."

It's a shame that the original Tipo 1308 1900 engine no longer survives, but this isn't uncommon in the case of racing machinery. Engines are blown up in competition, sometimes beyond repair, and they're usually replaced by whatever is "close enough" and available to make the next race. In this case, at least, it was a proper Alfa engine of the period. Fortunately, this car didn't end up with a small-block Chevy V-8 swapped underhood, as happened to all too many Italian thoroughbred machines over time. Because this car was being sold with several spare Tipo 1306 engines, a close cousin of the original 1308, the new owner could build up a solid-running powerplant.

The metal instrument panel wears a padded dash and minimal instrumentation, front and center to the driver. The carpets or rubber floor mats are long gone. Sporty red and black upholstery is a handsome offset to the silver exterior, and is presented as original to this car. Because this model was sold as an occasionally raced road car, its interior trimmings are a mix of sports-racing and luxury-car touches. Most factories wouldn't have bothered with two-tone upholstery or a padded dashboard in a pure racing car, but in this custom-bodied dual-purpose machine, the combination isn't at all unusual.

The original wire wheels are intact and in good condition. Many of these Alfa 1900s were originally equipped with steel wheels wearing chrome trim rings and hubcaps, but since this one is a very special Zagato model, the sportier wires are certainly the car's originals. Although not any stronger than the stamped steel wheels, the wires are likely a little lighter and thus preferable by drivers who enjoy a little track time.

Gooding & Company continues, "The interior is remarkably complete (save for missing carpets) and the original black and red upholstery treatment is presented as original.

"The bodywork is poorly aligned and has been painted with a combination of brushes and a spray cans, and the car was a non-runner as presented, so realistically, this rare and special Alfa needs and deserves nothing short of a full concours-level restoration. Amazingly, what appears to be the original tool roll, and most of the tools, are present. As are many bits of trim and chrome

that would be very difficult and expensive to find used or to otherwise replicate."

All in all, this is a spectacular barn find, a rare and desirable model in relatively whole and complete condition. The only things that could make it better, in my view, are if it wore the more desirable Zagato "double bubble" roofline bodywork, and if it still contained its original high-performance Tipo 1308 engine. Otherwise, it's the proverbial gem in the rough and absolutely worth saving and restoring at almost any cost.

The price for this particularly interesting piece of Italian sports car history, with an interesting ownership and military twist to it? A mere $1,012,000 with *at least* another half-million waiting to be spent on its restoration. This car was certainly bought by a savvy, astute enthusiast collector, and will make a superb show car or vintage racing machine.

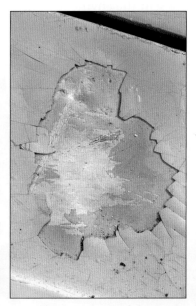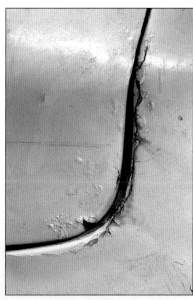

Left: *While worn and scarred, this car was remarkably complete, with all of the expensive-to-replace trim in place and in generally good condition.* **Middle:** *Some of the paint scars have never been touched up; it doesn't much matter, as this car will certainly be stripped to metal and refinished by its new owner.* **Right:** *This detail of the lower edge of the trunk panel evidences past minor damage and "quick and dirty" paint touch-up work; not at all uncommon on racing cars where a little bump-and-run action takes place on the track, and then is hastily touched up in between races. None of these past injustices will survive the body being stripped to metal, and the results of a full concours-level restoration.*

Chapter 7

1955 Mercedes-Benz 300SL Gullwing

ONLY JAY LENO COULD FIND, BUY, AND DO THIS

All photos courtesy of Wesley Allison and Matt Stone.

For some, that dream barn-find car is a Ferrari of one stripe or another. For others, maybe it's a Bugatti, Packard, or Duesenberg. This story is about another iconic automotive high watermark: a Mercedes-Benz 300SL coupe, also known as the mighty Gullwing. And only a guy such as Jay Leno, one of the world's most engaging and best-known motorhead collector/enthusiasts, could find it, buy it, give it a deep cleaning and sensitive mechanical recommissioning, and then take it out any time he likes and drive the wheels off it.

"I found this car locked up in Anaheim," Leno says. "It was raced extensively in the 1960s, and the guy damaged the engine. He claimed to have sent the engine to Mercedes to be rebuilt and, well, you know how that goes. We opened up the engine that came with the car

and saw evidence of fresh parts and assembly lube, so we hoped for the best.

"On the dyno, it ran great and made good horsepower, and so far so good.

"The car had a wonderful Southern California hot-rod appeal. It was painted this candy red by hot-rod and show-car legend Junior Conway and has a custom leather interior by the late Tony Nancy, another local hot-rod, show-car, race-car icon, plus it has a roll bar of unknown origin. We, of course, kept all that and cleaned up the car visually and mechanically. It's a joy to drive and runs great. It's fun to take to car shows because I don't worry much about it. People always have lots to say about all the missing hunks of paint, but if their kid bumps up against it, he's certainly not going to hurt it."

Imagine that: a beater Gullwing. Or, more accurately, a driver Gullwing. Leno worked at a Mercedes-Benz dealer when he was a kid, and adds, "You can't imagine the impact this car had at the time. Just look at the specs: born of a race car, overhead cam engine, mechanical fuel injection, and those outrageous doors. It was every bit as exotic in its day as any Ferrari, Lamborghini, or McLaren road car is now. It was really the first postwar exotic car, if you don't count the earliest Ferraris, which had more cylinders, but weren't any more technically advanced than the 300SL. And the quality. Other cars just weren't built like this back then. Everything was well engineered and beautifully made."

Leno continued, "And, fortunately, you can buy nearly every part on it. Stuff's expensive, but they have it through the Mercedes-Benz Classic Center. Buy a new fender for this car, and it fits with very little work. Buy a replacement panel for some other cars, and then

Benz out of the box: Jay Leno is on the phone to an unknown "lifeline" as the car is extracted. Luckily the hood and the rebuilt original engine weren't far away.

The 3.0-liter mechanically injected straight-6 was also highly exotic for its day, using a variety of metals in its construction. Note that the engine was laid on its side by several degrees, to make room for the induction system, as well as for the hood to close flush without large bubbles or scoops to accommodate the intake.

The original race number bubbles are rather worn and tired, further evidence to the car's on-track past.

the body shop usually has to get to work trimming and hand-fettling it so it'll come close to fitting. That's the difference with a classic Mercedes."

Jay offers me the pilot's seat. I flip down the steering wheel, then "Twister" my stocky frame inside. I sit relatively tall, with short legs, and the Gullwing proves to be a made-to-measure fit for me. I just have to remember to duck a bit when closing that special door.

"Know how to cold start one of these?" he asks. Of course not, Jay; unfortunately, I don't own one. "It's simple: First you activate the fuel enrichment via a knob on the dash; ditto the auxiliary fuel pump." A twist of the key, and it fires right off and thrums with purpose.

The exhaust system consists of a well-worn muffler and a large thin-wall single tube exiting the driver-side rear of the car. We idle for a minute to warm the fluids, engage first gear, and pull away with no drama. This engine feels torque-rich (it has to be more than its rated 203 ft-lbs), and the fuel injection meters in the fuel with relative precision, so it's crisp.

After a half mile or so, Jay clicks off the enrichment and auxiliary pump. The engine clears its throat and feels ready for action. I drive conservatively as there's not much temp on the gauges yet, but after a while, Jay points to the far side of the tach and says to "give it some revs." Sure, boss, if I must.

We find a relatively traffic-free, country-type road not far from Leno's Burbank, California, Big Dog Garage and give the Gullwing some stick. No wonder this car took the world, and most racetracks, by storm in its day. This thing is fast by any standard, even now, although of course it wouldn't take on a new Z06 or its spiritual successor, the SLS AMG 63. Doesn't matter. Go deep with the throttle in lower gears and the exhaust system snorts and bellows,

Facing Page: *Happy guy, happy car. Leno's super-capable Big Dog Garage crew freshened up the mechanicals, cleaned up the car, and had the mystic Gullwing back on the road in short order. Still wearing its tired original paint, race numbers, and Tony Nancy leather interior, the SL likely looks a lot like it did when last raced several decades earlier. Note that Leno runs it with the rear bumper in place but without a front bumper; this is likely how it raced originally.*

The Gullwing boasts many trademark styling and design cues, among them this air exhaust duct at the leading edge of the rear window. Because the Gullwing doesn't have large, roll-down side windows as did most coupes of the day, a mechanism was needed to help fresh air circulate through the cabin; regardless of its function, it's still a great-looking touch today.

the rear end squats a few degrees, and this baby really goes. Most cars of the day didn't stand a chance against it.

The view through the curved windshield is breathtaking; the prowed fenders and hood look classic and terrific. You know you're at the wheel of something special; any drive in this car is an occasion. The view out back is good, too, thanks to lots of glass area. I'm keenly aware of every car around me, and how close each one is to our position. I'm worried for the welfare of Big Red's fabulous fenders, even if its owner isn't overly concerned.

The Gullwing is a wonderfully analog car. There's no computerized artifice. You know the throttle pedal is connected to the intake system and the engine, and that the 4-speed manual transmission's shifter is moving actual mechanical gears in the transmission, which sits just below it. There's no asking some computer for permission to drive fast. The brake pedal actuates the brakes. This is not only a car, it's a machine. A refined and damned sporty one.

The SL has a wonderfully supple ride quality: never mushy, always in control, with no danger to your dental work on less than butter-smooth roads. One contributing factor is the relatively high-profile rubber, from when tires were no more than glorified O-rings wrapped around an oversized wheel.

Leno points out the factory steel wheels and hubcaps, which look absolutely right on this car. "A lot of Gullwings were factory-fitted with Rudge knock-off wheels, and many have since been retrofitted with them. The knock-off aspect is cool, but did you know they're actually heavier than these?" Jay knows his stuff, and appreciates the steelies-and-caps' lower unsprung weight, even if it's a less racy look. The suspension is nicely calibrated for controlled compliance rather than hair-trigger responses.

Because of the SL's prodigious power, it's not only easy to make speed in this car, but also to carry it. The steering is linear and true, with meaty weighting, no kickback on rough stuff, and meaningful feedback from the road surface. There's a bit of body roll, but once the car takes its set, it tracks true and consistent. There are plenty of brakes, even though they're drums.

This is a superlative machine for covering big miles when you have lots of time, and especially when you don't. "I wasn't really lusting after a Gullwing," says America's favorite late-night talk-show host, now retired from that nightly gig after 22 years "because the car always looked heavy to me. I didn't realize how quick they are until I drove one." Unlike some high-strung exotics, the SL proves to be a vice-free, yet thrilling drive. It's precise yet forgiving, plus completely and properly Germanic.

"That's one of the things I love most about old cars: The driving experience among them is so different," Leno explains. "Drive a new BMW or Audi or whatever big luxury sedan, and if you couldn't tell the difference visually

The Gullwing's cabin is an artful combination of luxury and sports racing. As in any proper race car, from which the 300SL Gullwing stemmed, the two main and most important instruments are front and center behind the steering wheel. Ancillary controls are spread out across the dash. The steering wheel tilts away to allow more robust drivers easier access, while the narrow rodlike shifter, with its Bakelite shift knob, seems almost dainty compared to the rest of the car's more masculine nature. Regardless, it's a comfortable interior ready for the Mille Miglia or a run from Los Angeles to Boston.

or by the badges, you may or may not know which was which. They're all pretty quick, quiet, smooth, and comfortable. They all have the same gadgets on them now, and the difference in driving experience has been largely homogenized out of them. You want to try something really unique? Drive a steam car or a turbine. *That's different!"*

How does a famous guy like Jay Leno find the cars and motorcycles in his collection? Being the popular host of television's top talk show for all those years certainly didn't hurt. Jay said that, "The show was my internet. Sometimes I'd say something about some car or that I was looking for something, and the next morning the studio office was barraged with calls. Older folks often wrote letters and included photos. Sometimes they're offering 'just an old car' and sometimes it's something really special."

Leno doesn't buy at public auctions because he fears that some bidders might try to "run him up" on bids and prices. He's been known to cruise parking garages, and has scored some great cars that way. He's also bought via classified ads and *Hemmings Motor News*. And in case you're wondering, he doesn't sell. Ever. He has on occasion donated cars to causes or to be sold at auction for charity, but once a car makes it to his garage, it's likely there for the duration.

With a 300SL Gullwing, every drive is an occasion. And let's not forget, its beauty inspires a shortness of breath in most serious car fools, including me. Will Jay ever "restore" or repaint and replate this car back to pristine original or concours-level finish? He says it's not part of any current plan; too many other projects in the shop at the moment.

I bet it'll stay just as it is. Because Jay Leno likes it that way. And so do I.

My thanks to Jay Leno. You can tour his garage, car, motorcycle, and automobilia collection, and lots of other fun stuff, at Jaylenosgarage.com.

Jay Leno never appears more relaxed or at home than when knocking about his massive Big Dog Garage Complex of airplane hangars and industrial buildings that has become his own personal, and very private, museum. And he's no dilettante entertainer car guy either; he really knows his stuff. Here Leno demonstrates that his Gullwing's battle-worn paint is none too precious and he has no concern if "some drunk guy or a seven-year-old kid" walks by this machine at a car show and brushes up against it. You'll have to go a long way to find a guy who more thoroughly enjoys and understands his many cars and motorcycles.

On the road, where it belongs. The Gullwing is a joy to drive, and as fettled by Leno's crew, runs and drives as new with no bad habits. The very 1970s candy red paint has flaws visible from any angle with several hunks and patches missing, but the car shined up pretty well. The owner has no plans to ever repaint or otherwise restore it.

Chapter 8

1956 Fiat Series 306/2 Bartoletti-Bodied Grand Prix Transporter

ALL HAIL THE BIG BLUE BUS!

Some things in life impress and occasionally over-whelm you with their sheer physical presence. One is Shaquille O'Neal, all 7 feet, 1-plus inch and 325 pounds of him. Some would say that meeting Kate Upton has the same impact, if for philosophically similar yet anatomically different reasons.

Of course, vehicles can exude similar power and impact; take, for example, Billy Gibbons' *Cadzilla*, the fabulous Boyd Coddington–built 1949 Caddy custom. It's a large car in the literal sense, but its persona seems even larger than the physical thing itself. Stand on the tarmac at an airport and look up at a Boeing 747 or an SR-71 Blackbird spyplane, for another example of this concept. One more manifestation of this notion is Don Orosco's fabulously large, famously blue Fiat Bartoletti race car transporter.

Orosco is, by day, a real estate developer in the Monterey, Pebble Beach, Carmel areas of Northern California, and also a seriously big-time vintage racer and hot rodder. He has been collecting, restoring, and racing vintage Scarabs for some years. You may remember Lance Reventlow's Scarab carbuilding and racing concern. Young Reventlow, not unlike Carroll Shelby, felt that American ingenuity, carbuilding skills, and racing drivers were good enough to take on anyone in the world, so he founded Reventlow Automobiles Incorporated (RAI) in Southern California's Thunder Alley area (not far from where the Los Angeles International Airport is now) and set out to build world-class sports racers and ultimately Formula 1 machines, called Scarabs.

In 1948, at age 12, Reventlow was introduced first-hand to motorsport when his mother, Woolworth department store heiress Barbara Hutton, married Prince Igor Troubetzkoy who won the Targa Florio endurance

Above: *This great old Shelby American press photo shows the team parked on the streets of Rheims, France, a venerable racecourse where the Cobras ran with great success in the 1960s. (Photo Courtesy of Shelby American)*

Facing Page: *Unfortunately, this fabulous 289 FIA Cobra wasn't included in the auction block purchase price of the fabulous Fiat-based Bartoletti transporter. It would have looked right at home riding on top of it, as the big bus transported many of its Shelby American siblings all around Europe in the early 1960s.*

race in Italy that year. As a teenager, Reventlow's family money afforded him the latest in exotic cars that surely led to his further involvement in motor racing.

Legendary fabricators, hot rodders, and carbuilders Dick Troutman and Tom Barnes were members of the Scarab act in the early 1960s. The small-block Chevy-powered Scarab sports racers were beautiful and wildly successful; the Offenhauser-powered open wheelers were less so, but they all served notice that machinery that was designed, built, powered, and driven by Americans could compete with the very best from anywhere, and beat them.

Reventlow was a movie-star-handsome young blond known for dating Hollywood starlets. But he was a capable driver; and even more so was his hired gun, a then little-known sports-car pilot named Chuck Daigh. Daigh was wicked fast, and could hustle a big-bore sports racer

around Riverside International Raceway as quickly as any driver of the day, going wheel to wheel with America's other greats including Dan Gurney, Jim Hall, and 1961 Grand Prix champion Phil Hill.

Life as a Transporter

Italy's Fiat, like GMC, built all manner of truck and bus chassis, and a handful of its bus chassis were, in the 1950s, delivered to Bartoletti of Forti, Italy, a builder of unique and special-purpose industrial truck bodies. This particular 1956 model chassis, 306/2, was commissioned as a car hauler for the Maserati Grand Prix team for use during the 1957 and 1958 F1 seasons. It was designed to carry up to three cars; with large storage compartments on the side to hold extra parts, team uniforms, and loads of the supplies needed while traveling around Europe during the F1 season.

Ferrari had a similar hauler, painted red instead of Maserati's racing blue. Blue turned out to be the lucky color. Maserati won the Grand Prix world driver's title in 1957, with Argentine ace, five-time world champion Juan Manuel Fangio at the wheel of the legendary Maserati 250F racer.

After the 1958 Formula 1 season, Maserati began winding down its involvement in Grand Prix, and the big Fiat was sold to Reventlow Automobiles Inc., as its grand prix team transporter for 1960 and 1961. It's often included in the archival photos of many books and magazines covering the racing scene of that time period.

After serving the RAI team in Europe during those seasons, it was purchased by Reventlow's Thunder Alley neighbor, Carroll Shelby, in 1962. His intent was to transport his Shelby American team's Cobra Daytona coupes to Le Mans and other stops along the sports car world championship tour in Europe. Because the Cobra sports cars weighed more than the open-wheel Scarabs, Shelby added an extra rear axle for additional stability and load capacity.

Post–Shelby American, the transporter did car hauling in Europe with stints for Lotus, privateer David Piper, the British Ford GT40, the Renault team, and Alan Mann, Ltd. As if this esteemed career wasn't enough, the big Fiat rig earned a supporting role in Steve McQueen's seminal racing film *Le Mans*, which was filmed during the summer of 1970. The car played three roles in *Le Mans*: team transporter for Ferrari, Renault/Mirage, and Porsche (for which it wore the iconic Gulf blue and orange of the Porsche 917s). The truck had to be repainted three times depending on which team hauler it was portraying.

After its Hollywood acting career, Mike Shoen acquired the Fiat. Shoen owned one of the famous Cobra Daytona coupes, and figured that the historic truck was the logical transport for it and his other Cobras. The big rig, still wearing its phony red Ferrari team livery from the filming of *Le Mans* was pretty well worn out by this time, but the Shoen family owned the U-Haul Corporation, so dealing with large trucks was familiar.

The Fiat was transported to the United States, and soon cast aside in the Arizona desert. In the mid-1990s, a long, contentious Shoen family lawsuit over control of the family business tied up all property, including the truck, for some years. It eventually wound up as the property of Mike's brother, Joe.

There may not have been a barn around big enough to hold the old truck after its tenure on the film set of Le Mans *in 1970, so less sensitive members of the Shoen family cast it aside in a desert storage yard. (Photo Courtesy of DBO Racing)*

Rescue from the Desert

Enter Don Orosco in 2006. By this time, Orosco had assembled his fleet of Scarab racers, and what better way to move and display them than with the Reventlow Scarab team's original transporter. Orosco, who had built and restored numerous cars to show-winning condition, wasn't really prepared for the monstrous job of restoring the big Fiat. Such was its state upon his acquisition.

It was all there but in dreadful shape. Nearly every body panel was damaged, bent, or corroded. The basic chassis wasn't too bad, although it needed to be worked over and stabilized by an outside team of bus chassis experts. Orosco assigned himself the job of "conductor" with his own DBO Motor Racing team cued up for the restoration of their lives. Parts sourcing alone turned out to be a long, worldwide endeavor. Orosco visited what remains of the Bartoletti company, not expecting to find shelves of mid-1950s spare parts. And, of course, he didn't.

Orosco has built and restored some outstanding hot rods, and his own team of mechanics and fabricators was bolstered by another half dozen or so men of similar talents, as well as specialists who were brought in depending upon the job. In the beginning, the restoration of this 80,000-pound rig must have felt like raising and cleaning up the *Titanic*. But the talented crew persisted; what couldn't be fixed or refurbished was fabricated from scratch. Even the Bartoletti badges and logos were recast.

Time? Two years, and about 8,000 man-hours to finish. Cost? Orosco doesn't think about or talk about it because it doesn't matter. The finished product is breathtaking and ultimately irreplaceable.

The Fiat's basic mechanical aspects were the least of the job. The original powertrain had been replaced along the way with a more modern, 11.5-liter (that's about 700 ci for you big-block fans) Leyland turbocharged 6-cylinder industrial diesel and 5-speed automatic transmission, which needed not much more than a major service and mechanical recommissioning to get running.

It was the billboard-size bodywork that proved to be the biggest aspect of the job; most of the original paneling was stripped off to facilitate stabilization and restoration of the chassis and body framework, which was then refitted with virtually all-new panels, fabbed by hand from new sheet metal stock. Another major undertaking was a complete reglazing, as every original pane of glass had been shattered.

Amazingly, one pair each of Reventlow's and Daigh's RAI team driving overalls still hung in the truck's side storage bay. As they do today.

The quality of this restoration is dazzling, and Orosco credits his small team of artisans. "They did it all. I just

Where do you park an 80,000-pound transporter truck? The answer is, of course, "Anywhere you like." Here, the Big Blue Fiat is parked in downtown Monterey, California, during Car Week in August 2012. This was just before being sold at the RM Collector Car Auction for $990,000, a figure that is likely only a little more than the cost of the considerable restoration.

watched, coached, and wrote big checks," comments this justifiably proud owner. The truck looks authentic, absolutely clean and detailed everywhere you look, but not overly shiny or falsely chromed. It's at least as nice as it was the day it was built, and probably better, but not appearing fake or overdone in any way. Jaws drop at the sight of it.

After its two-year hiatus and makeover, the big Fiat enjoyed an impressive public coming-out party in the paddock at Laguna-Seca Raceway in August 2008. The vintage race attendees were wowed not only by Orosco's impressive collection of Scarabs, but also by the massive blue bus that used to haul the Scarabs around Europe, and now carries them on the Monterey Peninsula.

And, have you noticed that this particular hue resembles the medium metallic blue seen on so many Shelby Cobras over the years? I can't help but wonder if Shelby might have been inspired by this shade, as seen on Reventlow's Scarabs and team transporter. Remember, the truck was still painted this color when Shelby American acquired it from Reventlow in 1962.

The following day at Laguna, the Fiat and its precious Scarab cargo appeared on the famously well-manicured lawns of the Pebble Beach Concours d'Elegance. That's right: the Maserati/Scarab/Shelby/Lotus/Piper/Mann/ *Le Mans* Fiat Bartoletti grand prix transporter mixing in with the Rolls-Royces, Duesenbergs, Packards, and other

classics at the world's most important car show. And why not? It is as stunning, historically significant, and beautifully restored as any of them.

Once ensconced in the Bartoletti's massive car cavern, any valuable race car would surely be safe and secure for the long ride from Le Mans to a nearby port, and then by ship home to the United States for the Shelby American Cobra Daytona Coupe team's next run at Daytona, Sebring, or Watkins Glen.

Chapter 9

1956 Lancia Aurelia B24S Spider America

AND ALONG CAME A SPIDER

In the June 1993 issue of *Thoroughbred & Classic Cars* magazine, Brian Palmer wrote, "Ask someone today about Lancia and chances are that if they've heard of the name at all, they'll register lukewarm recognition for a tarted-up Fiat." Which is most unfortunate, because Lancia, for many years, was among the world's most sophisticated as well as committed engineering- and design-driven automotive marques. Exotic? Absolutely.

Lancia's history dates to the early 1900s and the company always produced innovative, well-engineered machines. Founder Vincenzo Lancia was a development driver and a factory racing driver for Fiat before venturing out on his own, and most of the company's success stemmed from his personal charisma, drive, and feel for the machinery. Lancia raced in Formula 1

prior to Ferrari, and during the 1950s, 1960s, and early 1970s, many of Lancia's models were considered positively exotic. They were often race and rally winners the world over.

Among the many factors that relighted Lancia's flame after World War II was the successful luring of legendary engine design engineer Vittorio Jano away from Fiat, and the development of an all-new line of post-war automobiles. Lancia had dabbled with its own V-8 engines as early as the 1920s, and later produced a sophisticated single overhead cam V-4.

The magic pearl for Lancia was a new-from-scratch all-aluminum overhead valve 60-degree V-6, born at 1,754 cc designed by Jano and design engineer Francesco de Virgilio. Much like the seminal small-block Chevrolet V-8, the Lancia V-6 was developed from a need for a passenger car engine; it would ultimately be enlarged and redesigned for use in numerous small and large cars, commercial vehicles, and motorsport, living many years, lives, and incarnations along the way.

The new engine's primary purpose was to power the Aurelia lineup of automobiles that came to market in 1950. Of the new two-door coupes, four-door sedans, and convertibles, the most elegant and desired among them was the Aurelia B24 Spider. According to classic car auction house Gooding & Company, "At the Brussels Motor Show in January 1955, Lancia unveiled the B24 Spider America. Based on the fourth-series B20 GT, the B24 Spider America shared the model's improved 2.5-liter V-6 engine and De Dion rear axle, but featured a shorter chassis and standard floor shift. With a top speed

Above: *If you didn't know this Lancia Spider wasn't a Ferrari, you might think it was; the sensuous bodylines are the work of Pininfarina, which clothed many an important Ferraris over the decades. This car, although filthy and a bit run down cosmetically, appeared to be in fine shape structurally, with no body rot or accident damage.*

Facing Page: *Barn finds at collector car auctions sales experienced a great year in 2014, when dusty, musty, sometimes rusty, and unrestored examples of great cars brought high prices. Here, the Lancia is in a very prominent location at Gooding & Company's Monterey, California, sale in August 2014. The company's specialists were very careful not to clean, detail, or polish the car in any way prior to its moment under the bright lights of the auction block.*

approaching 115 mph, the Spider America was among the best-performing open sports cars of its day."

All Aurelia Spiders were powered by 2,451-cc versions of the Lancia V-6. The 1956 model, as shown here, is rated at 118 hp. Pininfarina designed the Spider and also constructed the cars in its Turin-area factories.

Among the Aurelia lineup's roster of impressive technical innovations is a rear transaxle unit that combines the gearbox, clutch, differential, and inboard drum brakes; it is very effective at moving weight from the front end of the car to the rear for better handling and balance. The V-6 makes a lusty growl and is smooth with a satisfying, linear power curve, and its excellent mid-range torque makes for less rowing of the 4-speed manual transmission.

These cars are comfortable, and neatly walk the balance between pure sports car and grand tourer. All Aurelias boast high build quality, but the Turin-built open models are particularly well finished and detailed. Given their high level of technical sophistication, build quality, and rarity, it's doubtful that any of the open-bodied Aurelias were big money makers for Lancia, but they were an elegant, sporty showcase for the company's technical prowess, as well as Pininfarina's abilities to design and produce relatively limited production runs of specialty sports cars.

Surely among the most efficient and reliable of Italian sports car engines is the Jano narrow-angle Lancia V-6, in production for many decades powering a variety of vehicles. Lucky for the buyer of this car that its original, cast dual intake air cleaner is still on the car. This component can be found, but it is rare and expensive if a replacement is needed.

The Spider America dashboard is a padded-metal body-colored unit with all of the important instruments right in front of the driver. The original leather seats were preserved in remarkably good condition; this is extremely unusual for an open-topped car that's been in long-term, somewhat unprotected storage.

Auction house Gooding & Company offered this car as part of its August 2014 sale in Monterey, California. The history of this particular B24S ("S" is for "sinestra" or left, as in left-hand drive) is somewhat foggy, but the company represents that this was the first time that the car was offered at public sale. Apparently, it sat in secure storage for many years. It was very original, complete, and largely undamaged at the time of its removal from storage, and pre-sale estimates placed value at $900,000 to $1.1 million.

In the hands of skilled and sensitive mechanics and technicians, a thorough detailing and mechanical recommissioning is likely possible. However, Gooding & Co wisely submitted that the car is the perfect candidate for a ground-up and complete restoration. This is truly the only way to restore it to top running condition and concours-ready appearance.

What was the price for this unmolested, sound, and largely original Lancia, showing only about 51,000 miles on its odometer? It was $880,000 including fees and commissions, with dirt, surface rust, paint damage, and cat prints included at no extra charge.

Pininfarina was great with its treatment of small details such as this rear-fender gas door with a built in lock. Italian designers and coachbuilders are very sensitive and generally spare in their use of chrome trim and jewelry; some French carbuilders tend to lay the trim on with a trowel, and while the result is sparkly, some are just over the top.

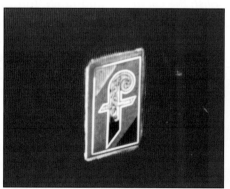

Left: The original VIN plate tells the story of this car's birth and place in the series of Spider production. Knowing an Aurelia's (or any classic car's) exact numbers and specs is very important, as in this case they were offered in a variety of body styles and evolutions. Its unlikely that an unscrupulous owner or restorer would attempt to rebody a less valuable B20 coupe into an Aurelia Spider, but making sure that all the numbers match is critical when the differences are measured in hundreds of thousands of dollars. **Middle:** This faded body emblem discloses that this car was designed and built at Pininfarina. The company was originally established by Giuseppe Farina as Stabilimenti Farina, then it was taken over by his son, Battista "Pinin" Farina. After World War II, the company was called Pinin Farina, and officially changed to Pininfarina in the early 1960s. **Right:** The original grille badge tells a bit of this particular car's life history, indicating that one of this car's early owners was a proud member of the Touring Club Italiano, an Italian sports car club.

The Spider America's rounded rump would have certainly looked appropriate on any Ferrari, Maserati, or Alfa Romeo of the era, with no messy convertible top structure to disrupt its lines, elegant bumpers, and small purposeful taillights.

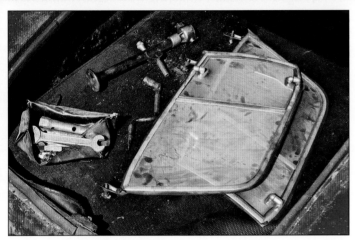

Left: *In this case, the all-important "junk in the trunk" included the difficult-to-replace side windows, some tools, and assorted trash. This is the stuff that's too often lost with many barn finds; paperwork, extra parts, accessories, tools, and even keys disappear throughout a car's life and travels, particularly in the case of long-stored and frequently moved non-runners. Be sure to look for and ask for these items when making a purchase; in many cases, the missing items sit in a box or on a shelf near where the car was stored. Don't leave them behind by forgetting to ask for them.*
Right: *Look hard enough in the paint on the trunk panel and you'll see a varied assortment of handprints, cat's paw prints, and lettering inscribed by the odd finger or two along the way. It's certainly part of the charm of selling a barn find "as found" and allowing the next owner to preserve this sort of patina, or strip it away for bodywork and fresh paint.*

Left: *Most Spider Americas were equipped with ancillary driving lights, similar to these, either by the factory, the selling dealer, or an enthusiastic owner.* **Middle:** *Some of these cars wear wire wheels, likely an option, but this one still has its original, factory-installed vented steel wheels and chromed hubcaps.* **Right:** *The rear-exiting dual exhausts tell a great story. The perfectly balanced Lancia V-6 isn't terribly loud but makes wonderful motor music as a smooth runner that revved relatively high for an overhead valve design of the time.*

Chapter 10

1956 Maserati A6G 2000 Zagato

FINDING THE MASERATI BEHIND THE WALL

Text by Matt Stone and Winston Goodfellow.
All photos courtesy of David Sydorick and Matt Stone.

By way of disclosure, I must mention that this car and its amazing story were previously featured in Tom Cotter's landmark book, *The Cobra in the Barn*. Given that Cotter and I have long-standing personal relationships with the car's owner, and that I had the chance to inspect the car personally and photograph it expressly for this volume, I elected to include it. That and the car's successful rescue from nearly impenetrable lockup storage in Sicily is kind of the thing that barn-find dreams are truly made of.

Maserati's A6G 2000 was at the forefront of the world's burgeoning, glamorous gran turismo scene during the Fabulous Fifties. The model debuted at 1954's Paris Auto Show and, thanks in part to its lusty, racing-derived 2-liter 6-cylinder engine and excellent agility, the jet set clamored to own one.

"The Maserati is just about the same wheelbase, height, width, and length as a Corvette," Walt Woron wrote of an A6G 2000 in the March 1957 issue of *Motor Trend*, "yet when these two tangle on a road course, the Corvette will have had it . . . In the corners, the Mazzy will leave the Corvette driver in a daze of tangled arms. In its class nothing can compare in roadability. . . ."

Further enhancing the A6G 2000's desirability was a chassis that lent itself to custom-made bodies, and Italy's leading carrozzerias were more than happy to oblige. The coachbuilders were then in the midst of an unparalleled boom of creativity. Their talented panel beaters earning less than 50 cents per hour made sure that the leading designers could continually put forth a stream of delectable creations. Companies such as Frua and Allemano provided opulent coupe and spyder bodies for the A6G 2000, each one different.

A third A6G 2000 coachbuilder was Ugo Zagato, and he took a different approach. Ugo Zagato was a talented craftsman and manager with a background in aeronautical construction who founded his Milan-based carrozzeria in 1919. Zagato's constant tinkering with aerodynamics and lightweight aluminum bodies made his designs a favorite among racers and performance-minded enthusiasts alike.

By the mid-1950s Ugo's son Elio was managing the firm and successfully racing Zagato products on the weekends, bringing in a number of orders in the process. The connection between coachbuilding and competition made it natural that Zagato would produce a small series of lightweight A6G 2000s. The company's lovely fastback design debuted in early 1955 and, over the next two years, another 19 were built. Like the Frua and Allemano creations, each was individually tailored to customer specifications.

That desire for uniqueness began to disappear in the late 1950s to early 1960s, as Maserati customers became

Above: *Tidy and perfectly proportioned from any angle, Zagato got this design absolutely right. The car wears just enough chrome trim to add surface detail to its clean, lithe lines and aluminum body panels.*

Facing Page: *David Sydorick's show-winning Maserati A6G 2000 Zagato is a stunner from any angle, looking fabulous again on the streets of Southern California.*

Right: *People have long been known to take extreme measures to store and protect their treasures, but building a brick wall between a car and the garage door is certainly unusual. As a DiNatale family member knocks away the last bricks that protected this jewel of a Maserati from potential thieves, this is what enthusiast David Sydorick saw. The dream was real, the car was as promised, and it was his.*

more interested in refinement rather than finicky individual cars. The new 3500 GT was selling in the hundreds each year, so the A6G 2000 quickly fell out of favor. Many fell into various states of disrepair, and those who could afford to keep them properly serviced were no longer interested in purchasing the previous model.

Three decades passed before the A6G 2000 once again became an "in" item. The late 1980s collector car boom had everyone scrambling, trying to find the next big thing. Barn-find stories abounded, tales of cars pulled out from years of hiding or hibernation only fueled everyone's enthusiasm to make the next big discovery.

Enter David Sydorick

One person lusting for such an adventure was David Sydorick. Born in Pittsburgh, by the 1970s Sydorick had found success on Wall Street where his financial acumen saw him rapidly climb the corporate ladder. In the mid-1980s his New York-based employer decided to open an office on the West Coast, and Sydorick landed in Southern California. He never looked back and his car collection blossomed in the process.

"As the years pass and a collection changes," Sydorick reflects today, "you finally figure out what it is you truly love. My passion is Italian carrozzeria, and for me that means Zagato. I just love the beauty and purity of their shapes."

Several drives on Italy's Mille Miglia brought the A6G 2000 Zagato to his attention. "I seem to fall for cars during the several days we race," he muses. "I enjoy watching something from the front and rear, to see it in action going up and down the hills and through towns.

"Another wonderful element of the Mille is the variety of people who get out of each car. Every time I saw a Maserati Zagato, the person driving it was an elegant Italian gentleman."

Sydorick soon found himself a member of this exclusive club when he bought chassis 2179, the class winner at 1996's Pebble Beach Concours d'Elegance, the year Zagato was featured.

But the more he researched the cars, the more he realized there was one A6G 2000 that remained undiscovered. For many years, chassis 2121 was owned by Sal DiNatale, the proprietor of a popular Los Angeles–based repair and restoration shop in the 1960s. Several Maserati books had alluring photos that highlighted 2121's unique-to-the-A6G Zagato signature "double bubble"

A justifiably proud Sydorick and the jewel-like Maserati take pride of place in his fabulous garage, with no brick wall to keep it from the sunshine ever again.

roof, single air intake, and California black plate.

The Southern California rumor mill was rife with stories that 2121 was stashed away in a garage in Sicily, DiNatale's birthplace. But as hard as he tried, Sydorick could never find any concrete information on its whereabouts.

Then, one fateful day in early 1997, two men called, asking if they could come by and see his car collection. One visitor was Maserati enthusiast Boris Subbotin, the other was the elusive Sal DiNatale. As they examined A6G 2000 chassis 2179 David mentioned in passing how much he admired 2121, then casually asked if it was actually in Sicily.

"Sal responded that indeed it was," Sydorick recalls. "He said he had planned to move back there and had shipped the car back to his hometown. He just never followed it back."

And that is when the fun started. "Everyone gets the thrill of the chase," Sydorick chuckles. "It was definitely there for me. After you have restored something and then used it, it is almost like, 'so what's next?'"

The Maserati Zagato Returns to California

Subbotin quickly understood Sydorick was the ideal owner for 2121, so over the next several months the two men quietly tried to convince DiNatale that David's multiple-car garage would be the ideal home,

This special Maserati still wears its original California black and gold license plates from its first tour of duty in Southern California decades before.

 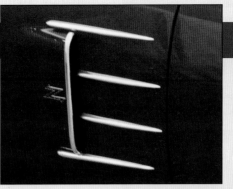 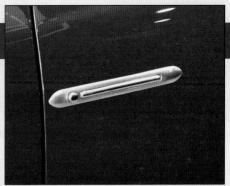

Left: *Borrani knock-off wire wheels and drum brakes drilled with cooling holes were common for Maserati racing and gran turismo machines of the era.* **Middle:** *Zagato's famous "Z" adorns the scoop-and-spears trim on each side of this valuable and highly sought Maserati.* **Right:** *The details are usually just right on most custom-bodied Italian cars, particularly those of Zagato and Pininfarina, such as this elegant, almost dainty pop-out door handle.*

where the Maserati would lovingly be restored. DiNatale's resistance finally melted after a year, and Sydorick suddenly found himself on an overnight Alitalia flight from Los Angeles to Milan, then Catania, Sicily. From there he drove to Taormina and checked into a hotel.

Sal's daughter met David that night, and they had a harrowing drive through a cold, blustery storm to Sal's birthplace, Savoca, where *The Godfather* was filmed. A walk through several of the town's dark, deserted alleys and walkways led them to a brick garage, filled with building supplies. They entered and Sal's daughter, after fumbling through the darkness, found what she was looking for. She tugged on a tattered hanging string and a solitary, low-wattage light bulb dangling from the ceiling popped on.

The wind howled outside, easily drowning out Sydorick's chilled but happy sigh. The Maserati Zagato silently stared back at its new owner.

The two returned the next morning to find a crowd standing in the swirling mist; it seemed that all of Savoca knew an American was coming to remove the old car from the garage. The door opened and the crowd instinctively moved forward for a better look. A two-foot brick wall stood behind the Maserati, there to slow down any thieves.

As Sal's son-in-law hammered down the wall, Sydorick digested what had fueled his fire for so many months. The 2121's paint was stripped, the tires were flat, the Plexiglas windows were slightly cracked from age, but it was all there: "double bubble" roof, single hood scoop, and California black plate, just as the books had shown. While examining the all-original interior Sydorick found California registration statements from 1959 and 1960!

When the brick wall was down, the tires were inflated and the Maserati was pushed out in the street, seeing daylight for the first time in two decades. The crowd moved back, and 2121 was loaded onto a truck for the first leg

of a long journey back to California. Sydorick soon followed, exhausted but elated.

The delectable Maserati made its public debut three-and-a-half years later at 2002's Pebble Beach Concours d'Elegance, its three-year frame-off restoration finished just days before. David was like an expectant father, nervously scanning the field. He knew the competition would be tough. His class boasted a number of superbly restored cars, including two rare Aston Martin DB4 Zagatos from the early 1960s.

As the judges approached Sydorick he was certain they might question its unique features, something that might affect its score. No sooner had he started his explanation than lead judge John Ling said, "Relax, David. I used to drive this car all the time to get parts when I worked for Sal!"

The Maserati Zagato won its class.

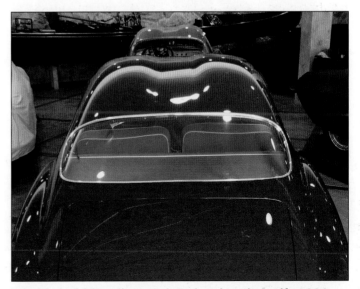

Double bubbles all around! Sydorick's silver Alfa 1900 also wears a Zagato body; both it and the Maserati share that coachbuilder's iconic "double bubble" roofline.

Chapter 11

1956 Maserati A6G 2000 Allemano

SAME GREAT A6G, DIFFERENT SUIT

All photos courtesy of Kirk Gerbracht.

Many things make this tidy Maserati coupe an extra-special barn find. It is a very rare and highly sought-after model; its entire ownership history is known and documented, and it wears handsome Allemano coachwork. Moreover, even though faded and dusty, it was apparently stored with some care, has suffered little damage, and is highly complete. This is an all too rare condition in the world of barn finds, where dust and a little rust are common, but so are massive body damage and water pooling in the floorpans, as well as parts removed and stored in boxes (or not) all over any given barn, garage, or shed.

This example, chassis 2165, while hardly perfect, is highly original, still bearing its original numbers-matching engine and transmission. As presented for sale at its January 2015 Scottsdale auction by Gooding & Company auctioneers, this car was deliciously complete.

Even though this particular example is a pure and street-legal car, its parentage stems from the racetrack. The basic architecture of its engine, a dual overhead cam 1,986-cc twin plug, all-aluminum straight-6 good for 160 hp, stems from a design by Gioacchino Colombo, famous for, among other things, the design of the Ferrari 3.0-liter V-12 "Colombo" engine. The Maserati's engine, as factory installed in this car, wears triple Weber carburetors, wet-sump oiling, and a full exhaust as befitting a high-performance street machine. A street engine, yes, but highly exotic to be sure.

Further evidence of its specification as a road-going gran turismo is the fact that this car wears full bumpers, road lights, leather-trimmed interior, and full instrumentation. It's quite handsome in its factory color combination of racing red with a red and black interior. I don't know anything about the original owner, Julius Byles, who bought the car new in Turin, Italy, in 1956, but it is obvious that he was a man of some financial substance and impeccable taste to have selected and specified this example.

The car lived most of its first decade in Italy. In the mid-1960s it was imported to the United States for a Mr. Levy, in Connecticut; he sold the car to a Mr. Ridgewood in New Jersey a mere two years later. After another two years, it was sold to a Mr. Thiemann of Pennsylvania, who kept it a decade before selling it to a Mr. Larkin

GOODING &COMPANY

Above: *The wheelbase is relatively long, as are the doors and the greenhouse, indicating this as a 2+2 body style, with adequate, if not lavish, room for a back seat. Its longer rear overhang allows for a reasonably sized trunk. What a great machine to take to your chalet in the Alps for a weekend getaway in 1956. Or 1966. Or 2016.*

Facing Page: *Allemano certainly got the lines and proportions right on this tidy Maserati 2+2. The front overhang is relatively spare, giving a long and elegant dash-to-axle ratio. It was a handsome machine in 1956, and is equally so today. This car's A6G 2000 underpinnings also proved to be successful in racing, and gave this primarily street version considerable performance for the day. This great example showed relatively clean body panels, gaps, and shut lines.*

of Massachusetts. At this point the car was taken off the road and put into long-term storage. Gooding & Company's consignor previously acquired the car from that Massachusetts owner.

When you think of Maseratis bodied by Allemano, many people first think of the Maserati 5000 GT model of the 1960s; most, but not all, of those were Allemano bodied. Of the 60 A6G 2000 chassis produced by Maserati, only 21 wore Allemano bodies. Maserati had no exclusive body provider then; it's common to see 1950s and 1960s Maseratis wearing a wide variety of coachwork from Allemano, Frua, Ghia, Pininfarina, Touring, Monterossa, Zagato, and others.

What makes it so attractive from a barn-find standpoint is its completeness; all of its original equipment and hard-to-find pieces of trim are intact. Gooding &

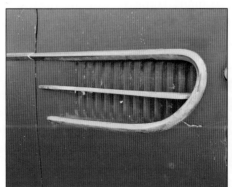

Left: *The original wire wheels are intact although they are deeply pitted and will require restoration and truing to be safe again for road use. Notice the cooling ventilation holes in the factory brake drums. This technology likely stemmed directly from Maserati's racing experiences with this same chassis architecture.* **Middle:** *Note the artful detailing in the swoopy chrome trim surrounding the front fender exhaust vents. Fortunately, all of the difficult-to-find and expensive-to-replace trim bits on this car are present.* **Right:** *All factory VIN and build plates are aboard and clean. When bits like this go missing, it's difficult to prove what the car is and what its numbers are. The fact that the screws holding these plates to the machine-turned aluminum firewall appear to have no scratches or score marks in them, as well as having a light coat of corrosion, suggests that they've never been removed or swapped from another car. (This highly unethical practice not only goofs up the provenance of many cars, but is also a federal offense.)*

The car's slim window pillars might fool you into thinking it's a Pininfarina or Ghia design, rather than an Allemano. This is the look that Allemano later developed for the lush, custom-built, and very expensive (both then and now) Maserati 5000 GT. Trim and ornamentation on the A6G 2000 is rather spare and elegant, so the jewelry doesn't overwhelm the car's clean and elegant lines.

Company noted that the car was being offered including the original instruction manual, (last owner) Larkin's Maserati Club membership card, and copies of the Maserati factory build record.

The car also still wears period registration stickers and a dealer-installed optional Condor Electronik radio. Of equal fortune is that its never suffered from the small-block Chevrolet V-8 engine swap inflicted on so many Ferraris and Maseratis of the day. This engine swap was common

when the original engine was damaged, the owner desired increased performance, or the owner just grew tired of the maintenance needs of the original engine.

Obviously, the carpets are faded, the upholstery is hard, and surface rust coats most of the chrome trim. This car could be mechanically recommissioned and sympathetically restored to a high-level drive condition without the need for a complete nuts-and-bolts restoration. It would, of course, be the ideal candidate for a full concours restoration, since it is so complete and original.

Gooding & Company experts predicted that the car would sell for $750,000 to $950,000. It fell just short of that, crossing the block at $715,000 including fees and commissions. If another $285,000 is invested to bring the car back up to snuff, it will be one handsome and rare million-dollar baby.

I wouldn't suggest taking a knock-off hammer to these lock nuts without first soaking them in a lot of penetrating oil. A little heat from a torch might also be needed to knock the ears off without damaging the underlying threads. Fortunately, the wheels appear to be complete and unbent, and a qualified wheelwright and restoration expert will have them sparkling, balanced, and trued without too much hassle.

The car lived most of its later life in Pennsylvania, having been taken off the road in 1969–1970, as evidenced by this old Pennsylvania plate and a similarly dated registration sticker still affixed to the windshield, indicating its most recent licensing in that state. These great bits of documentation add provenance, and help to tell the car's history and path through time.

Top Left: *Looks like a comfy place for a cross-continent tour, with 2+2 seating, full carpeting, and a well-equipped dash. Colors and materials are correct, although the original fabrics, upholstery, and rubber are hard and dry. It will need either a deep cleaning and much reconditioning, or replacement.* **Top Right:** *The original alloy-and-wood steering wheel is in generally good shape except for some minor cracking covered up by a bit of hastily applied electrical tape. Instrumentation is complete and comprehensive; note the optional, dealer-installed radio at the far right.*
Bottom Left: *The il Tridente badge and the sweetheart-shaped grille surround identify this as a Maserati. Even though one owner's decision to paint the bumpers flat black was a stylistic faux pas, the black paint likely preserved the chrome and underlying metal from the ravages of time and rust. Amber-lens foglights are also a non-factory installation.* **Bottom Right:** *The mildly detuned 2.0-liter street version of Colombo's Maserati straight-6; in racing tune it would have had a dry-sump oiling system, larger carbs, and likely more aggressive cam timing. This engine puts out plenty of lusty, reliable power and will run as smoothly as any other thoroughbred straight-6.*

Chapter 12

1956 Mercedes-Benz 300SL Gullwing

AUTOMOTIVE HIGH-WATER MARK?

The original Mercedes 300SL Gullwing coupe is without doubt one of the greatest among classic sports cars. It was born of racing, and is a fabulous piece of design work. Moreover, it boasts those impossibly cool gullwing doors. The first 300SL was a classic the day it was built, and its reputation and status in the collector car community has been burnished to a higher gloss ever since. They were very high-tech, exotic cars for their day, and remain so now.

Some were bodied in aluminum, many were raced, and they were bought by Hollywood, political, and motor racing royalty. Only about 1,400 were built, and they've become valuable and much sought after in today's fervent classic car market. The mechanical and technical reasons for the 300SL Gullwing's brilliance was discussed in great detail in Chapter 7, covering the discovery, mechanical recommissioning, and my drive of Jay Leno's candy red 1955 model, so I won't repeat all the specs and oily bits here.

A winner by any measure.

Of all the cars anyone could wish to discover locked away in a barn or garage after decades, a Gullwing has to be high on the list. This off-white 1956 model has no celebrity history, as such, and it doesn't wear the rare aluminum coachwork. But it enjoyed an interesting early life, was locked in storage for decades, and remained in single-family ownership for more than 50 years.

The 1956 Mercedes-Benz 300SL chassis number 198.040.5500624 was delivered new, early in that year, to a German industrial designer, Fredrich Stuckenbroker of Hamburg, Germany. Herr Stuckenbroker kept the car for just over a year before selling it to Dr. Harry Kaplan of Brooklyn, New York. At the time that the car made its transatlantic voyage from Europe to New York is likely when the original European kilometers-per-hour speedometer was replaced with a U.S.–spec miles-per-hour gauge.

Left: *All of the original badging, chrome, trim, and detail pieces remain on the car. These are things that all too often disappear when a car is stored for long periods of time, or parked in an unsecured barn. No such problem with this car.* **Middle:** *The original data plate confirms the model number with the chassis number stamping just below it. Mercedes-Benz production records and documentation are immaculate and highly detailed; the company can determine the where, when, and specification for virtually any car it produced.* **Right:** *The white repaint is showing signs of wear and age; it has been scarred and patched in several places. If you fancy a "beater Gullwing" in your garage, this would be a fine example to add to your collection.*

Dr. Kaplan kept the car for several years more than did its original owner, before he sold it to nearby New Jersey architect Helmut Geiger. Geiger kept, owned, and drove the car for some years, and it was retained by his family until only recently, when it was removed from storage and sold to an (undisclosed) owner who then consigned it to Gooding & Company's Pebble Beach auction sale in August 2014.

The car led an active early life, and was featured in several magazines and other publications. It made concours d'elegance and Mercedes-Benz club car show appearances during the early and mid-1960s. The car was originally painted silver at the factory, with a blue leather and plaid cloth interior. Geiger painted the car off-white.

Some Sports Car Club of America (SCCA) stickers are in one of the rear windows, but it is not clear whether Geiger himself raced this car or was merely an SCCA member, although documentation shows that he ran the car at a few Mercedes-Benz club track events in the mid-1960s. Even so, it appears that this owner drove the car actively through the 1960s. Then the car was put into long-term dry storage, which explains its well-worn patina but lack of rust, dampness, or corrosion, except for a dusty, musty-smelling interior.

This magnificent Gullwing can be approached in a couple of different ways. One would be a thorough mechanical recommissioning along with a comprehensive detailing job, and then to drive and enjoy the car as is. This isn't a bad alternative because the car is genuinely patinated and has a glow of time, use, and enjoyment. Because the driver-side door is a little sprung and doesn't close properly, some skilled body and panel alignment is in order to make the car drivable. A downside of this approach is that the car was repainted and doesn't wear its original paint or colors, so you'd be preserving less of its originality, but more of its specific life history.

Of course, the other avenue is to disassemble and fully or partially restore the car to original spec, colors, and condition.

I don't know what course a new owner will follow because the car didn't sell at the auction that day in August of 2014. Gooding & Company's preliminary pre-sale estimate was $1.4 to 1.8 million, and the car failed to reach that level, so it was declared a "no sale." Its search for a new owner, and the path back to roadability, continues.

The silver-painted dash and instrument panel confirm this car's original color combination; if the car were originally white, the metal dash and panel would also be white. The blue Tartan cloth is factory original, and although it is in need of a thorough shampoo job and replacement of the aged, slightly collapsed seat foam, it looks good and would still be serviceable if the next owner is inclined to keep it.

Facing Page: *Looking slightly worn but still handsome, this fabulous Mercedes-Benz drew considerable attention from bidders and onlookers alike. It is very complete, and sits on the proper stock steel wheels with hubcaps and trim rings. Even though not original to this car, the current white over dark blue color combination makes a convincing statement for not tearing it down for a complete restoration. This amazing machine remained in single-family ownership for more than five decades, although it was locked away in storage for a good portion of that time.*

Chapter 13

1958 Porsche 356A Speedster

GREAT CAR, GREAT OWNER, GREAT STORY

All photos courtesy of Kirk Gerbracht.

The 356A Speedster is one of the 1950s' most sought after Porsches. And what's not to like; it has that sexy, lightweight body style and a cabin stripped of all non-essentials. The pinnacle of this model is the Speedster Carrera, which ran the racing-derived twin-cam Carrera engine, although most Speedsters were powered by versions of the 1,600-cc overhead valve horizontally-opposed air-cooled 4-cylinder engine. The base version of this powertrain was called the "Normal" and the higher-output version was dubbed the "Super."

The cars were popular street sports cars when new, and proved to be highly successful on the racetrack too. Steve McQueen bought one new (his first new car) and won his first SCCA race aboard it at Santa Barbara in 1959. The faded silver example shown here led a less glamorous, yet still most interesting life, prior to its offering at auction by Gooding & Company at its Arizona sale in January 2015. In preparation for auction,

Gooding & Company shared the car's history: "In June 1958, Ken Johnson purchased a shining silver metallic Porsche Speedster for the then-princely sum of $3,641 and drove it to his family home in Long Beach, California, where it remained for the next 56 years.

"A veteran of the Korean War, Mr. Johnson cruised in his Speedster throughout Southern California, competing in beach volleyball tournaments, as well as up the coast on daily trips to Malibu while attending Pepperdine University. His wife Ilene recently recounted many fond memories of trips taken in the Speedster, including one special evening in 1961 when Ken proposed marriage while she sat in the passenger seat, alongside the Pacific Coast Highway.

"In 1972, the Speedster developed engine trouble when returning from a trip to Big Sur and, rather than accept a rebuilt replacement from his local shop, Mr. Johnson had his Speedster's original engine rebuilt and reinstalled. There was no way to know how important this decision would be decades later.

"As the years passed, Mrs. Johnson asserted that she would continue to ride in the Speedster only if her husband made it more comfortable. As a result, cabriolet-style seats were installed along with a Dynaplastics accessory hardtop with Plexiglas side curtains. The original red Speedster bucket seats, dry from many years of storage, accompany the sale of the car.

"Mr. Johnson passed away in September 2014, with his Speedster tucked away in the same garage that it was first parked in 1958. Protected by a heavy cover and beneath layers of various household items long since cast aside, the Speedster remained behind a garage door that had been nailed and screwed closed to deter would-be thieves. When the door was finally opened in

Left: *Many Speedster owners chose either to remove their car's bumpers entirely for a racier look, or perhaps just the bumper guards and overrider bars. Luckily, this owner left all that hardware intact, further preserving the car's originality. Even more surprising is that the original front license plate and dealer frame are still intact.* **Middle:** *The interior shows signs of honest use and enjoyment. It will certainly require some restoration work, but could be made very presentable with detailing and tidying. Note the rare Motorola "Valumat" AM radio, and that one of the registration tags is held in place around the steering column by an old spring-loaded registration holder, commonly used in the 1960s.* **Right:** *Among the many cool touches of originality on this car are its original California "black and gold" license plates, as well as the chromed metal license plate frames from legendary Vasek Polak's Porsche dealership in Redondo Beach, California. Polak built and sponsored many famous racing efforts, and gave several young and later famous drivers their start in motorsport. The "PRE 501" plate number has no particular meaning; it is from long before you could order vanity plates in California.*

September 2014, 83870 rolled out into the sunlight for the first time in decades.

"In the following weeks, the Porsche received new tires, a six-volt battery, brake and fuel system servicing, and the carburetors were resealed. Soon after, the Speedster was serviced and subsequently the engine was started; the car has logged several test miles prior to sale.

"As expected, the engine and trunk lids bear clear stampings, the door skins resound with a lovely metallic echo when tapped, and the doors close with the unmistakable ring of an unrestored car.

"Today, 83870 has rejoined a world far more appreciative of its design and rarity than when it was last driven. Bearing the signs of over half a century's existence, it is surely among the last sequestered Speedsters left to be rediscovered and would be an incredible sight on the road in its current condition. At the same time, there is no question that its lifelong Southern California residency makes it an incredible prospect for a top-level restoration by a discerning new owner."

Indeed! Gooding's pre-sale estimate was $275,000 to $375,000, and the little Porsche blew the lid off that range in a hurry, as the bidding sprinted well past $200,000 in mere moments, finally settling at $484,000. It's a great,

highly original car with single-family ownership, living and stored in a dry Southern California environment. Moreover, high demand and good marketing translate into big bucks. Another example of a barn find done right.

The original 1600 Normal-spec engine was temporarily replaced by another unit, but was rebuilt and reinstalled along the way. A thorough mechanical recommissioning should have this Speedy back on the road in no time. Although 60 hp doesn't sound like a lot these days, it was enough to move the flyweight Speedster along with brio, and to many SCCA race wins. Racing actors James Dean and Steve McQueen both owned them.

Facing Page: *This is the unmistakable profile of an original late-1950s Porsche Speedster. Its Reutter bodywork looks very similar to that of other 356 models of the era, but the Speedster badge on the side, plus that impossibly low cut front windshield, are the immediate tells of Porsche's lightweight sports roadster conceived primarily for the North American market. This one wears a rare and unusual aftermarket Dynaplastics hardtop, which somehow compliments the Speedster low-slung lines, even though most visualize this car running topless. You might wonder why the "baby moon" style hubcaps don't wear the expected Porsche logo crest, but these pieces are correct and accurate for this year and model car. The seminal Raydot rearview mirror would have been chrome, instead of painted black.*

Chapter 14

1958 Ferrari 250 GT Ellena

PIECES, PARTS, BOXES, AND TIN CANS

All photos courtesy of Eddie Montini.

Among the many great Ferraris produced during the late 1950s, the 250 GT Boano and Ellena coupes aren't well known or often thought of. This is a shame, because they are beautiful and a joy to drive, and are truly representative of early Ferrari 250 GT coupes. The body design is of course from Pininfarina, and Ferrari ultimately subcontracted the body construction to Carrozzeria Boano located near Turin.

Boano built a good number of the cars, and then when Mario Boano left his company to lead Fiat's styling department, the business was taken over by his son-in-law, Ezio Ellena, and the firm's name was changed to Carrozzeria Ellena. Thus the early examples are referred to as Ferrari 250 GT Boanos, and, logically, the later cars are called 250 GT Ellenas.

With the exception of minor design changes and ongoing mechanical evolutions, they are substantively the same car, and equal members of the Ferrari 250 gran turismo coupe family. Power for all comes from Ferrari's seminal Colombo 2,953-cc (3.0-liter) single overhead cam V-12. In this installation it wears a trio of Weber carburetors, is rated at 250 hp, and is backed by a 4-speed manual transmission. This model, particularly in profile, resembles the somewhat more famous 250 GT Tour de France.

The more aggressive Tour de France was also a successful racing car; in fact, many Boano- and Ellena-bodied 250 GTs have been rebodied as Tour de France models. It is a sad fact that for some years, "lesser" known and less expensive Ferraris, such as these Ellena and Boano coupes, as well as others such as the 2+2 250 GTE, were often scrapped for their powertrains and chassis, to be rebodied as "tribute models" or more accurately as fake examples of the most collectible and expensive Ferraris, including the 250 GTOs and 250 GT Spyder Californias.

Fortunately, as these "lesser" models have become prized for their own intrinsic value and appeal, their prices have risen dramatically, and that previous unthinkable trend seems to have died off.

This particular 250 GT Ellena, chassis 0855 GT, has a unique history. Arizona's Eddie Montini is deep into big-time GM muscle cars, particularly Yenko-edition Chevrolets. In 2004, he was introduced to another local enthusiast who wanted to visit his toy box and see his rare Chevys. Montini didn't really think of himself as a "Ferrari guy" but happened to be the original owner of a 1966 Ferrari 330 GT. His guest noticed the car up on the service rack, and asked Montini if he'd have any interest in an earlier, 250-series Ferrari. As any of us would, Montini said, "Tell me more."

The visitor said he knew a "friend of a friend" who'd had a Ferrari 250 coupe since the mid-1970s, and might be inter-

Left: *Not exactly a barn, but in this case, a large trailer painted barn red will have to do. The big metal box actually made a good storage place for the Ferrari, because it's mostly air- and watertight, with no dirt floor as found in many barns. It was also secure from prying eyes and crowbars, keeping the rare body and parts from walking away in the middle of the night. And finally, it was an easy way to move the car when necessary. New owner Montini used a forklift and lots of muscle to unpack all of the contents and move them into his own trailer for transport to Arizona.* **Right:** *The risk of a disassembled car traveling around the country is that parts may go missing along the way. That occurred in this case; the wheels, hubs, shocks, and countless other bits disappeared. Fortunately, care had been taken to crate up as much as possible, and keep those boxes with the car wherever it went.*

ested in selling it. The car was disassembled and packed into a storage trailer with most of its parts in crates. The friend got in touch with the 250's owner, who along with the car, lived in the hills outside Reno, Nevada. He asked about the car's status and the plans for it. The Ferrari owner had had the best of intentions to restore the car, but he was getting on in years, and at some point decided the job was now a bit beyond him.

So yes, the car was for sale, but only to the right party: someone discrete and qualified to redo the car properly. Montini and the Ferrari owner agreed on a plan to meet, talk about, and see the long-stored Ferrari.

Montini recalls the whole process was a little spooky and that the car's owner, Mr. Daniels, was a total character, although he obviously knew cars, and was well versed in his Ferrari's history. They met at a nearby casino because Daniels wasn't ready to divulge the location of his home or the car; moreover, he arrived at the meeting *armed*. Montini says he felt as if he were being interviewed for a job. It turned out that Daniels' home was in a rather deserted area, "way off the grid," recalls Montini. The nearest neighboring home was a considerable distance away.

They finally arrived at the remote location; among the various buildings and vehicles on the property was a huge barn-red trailer container. It was parked so close to another structure that Daniels had to hitch up a semi-truck to move it so the rear of the trailer could be opened.

The handsome Ellena coachwork was visible far in the back of the trailer, nearly obscured by four large wooden crates of its parts. The car, which had been fully stripped of its powertrain, suspension, and interior, as well as several paint jobs, sat in the trailer, as promised, covered by a cheap blue plastic tarp. The one thing Montini didn't see was the car's engine.

Strangely, the engine was packed in a separate wooden crate, stored in the garage, not in the trailer with the car and the rest of its parts. The engine had become separated from the chassis at some point and was sent to a shop in New York to be rebuilt. The job was done, the engine crated for shipping, but the bill went unpaid. The shop then decided to hold a lien sale to cover the unpaid bill. Luckily (or oddly) enough, the person who bought the engine was one of 0855's previous owners so the missing engine was almost magically reunited with

Facing Page: *Arizona here we come: Dollied up and ready for a road trip. You'd never mistake these bodylines as coming from any era other than the 1950s. The "reverse" cut of the B-pillar lines is softened by the large, steeply curved (but missing) rear window; the vestigial fins are also pure 1950s. The next time this car pulls into a trailer, it should be for a great concours somewhere, and it will assuredly be under its own power, riding atop a quartet of Borrani wire wheels.*

its original chassis. What a stroke of luck for the Ellena and its potential future owners. By coincidence, Montini noticed that Daniels had a rare Porsche 914/6 parked in his garage near the Ellena's engine.

The car was torn down to the last nut, bolt, and washer. However, more than a few important things were missing, such as all five of the original Borrani wire wheels, knock-off spinners, and hubs, as well as the rare Houdaille shock absorbers. The car had been all over the United States during its lifetime, and apparently lost a few parts along the way; Montini recalls about 40 large coffee cans full of nuts, bolts, trim, and bits that went along with the deal.

Montini was unable to close the deal during that first Nevada visit and exhumation, but after a few weeks of conversations, an agreement was struck, and Montini bought the car. He recalls that it took a large trailer, several helpers, and a lot of grunting and groaning to get everything packed up and trucked back to his Arizona home.

Montini is a very particular guy, and likes his cars absolutely right, and factory authentic. So he's done a fair amount of pecking around the Ferrari to verify its original specs, equipment, and colors. After lots of sleuthing, he's uncovered remnants of black, silver, and blue paint all over the car. The dashboard appears to have been black, indicating that the Ellena's exterior was originally black as well. Wanting to stick to the car's period-correct color palette, he's going to restore it to either black or one of

After the forklift-required removal of a couple crates of heavy Ferrari parts, and the removal of a cheap blue tarp, the Ellena happily showed its tail to Eddie Montini, who eagerly sought its rescue from the big red box. The body was found in generally good shape, except for some rear-end accident damage. Fortunately, renowned Ferrari parts man Tom Shaughnessy came to the rescue with a clean clip and replacement panels from another totaled Ellena so the body can be properly restored with clean factory metal where needed.

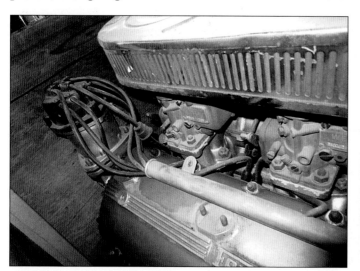

Left: *Once the crated engine was found in the garage, not the trailer, it was a relief to see matching serial numbers, and that the V-12 was largely complete. This included difficult- and expensive-to-replace parts such as the factory intake manifold, trio of Weber carbs, proper air-filter housing, and the right dual distributors. Building this engine from a bare block would have been a major undertaking just to ensure that all of the factory-correct components were sourced and used.* **Right:** *Luckily for the new owner, the engine is complete and correct, showing modest evidence of having been overhauled. It is clean on the outside with no evidence that it's ever been fired and shows a fresh gasket sealer here and there. But just to make sure it's shipshape inside, he plans to tear into it to repair and replace as needed, which is a relatively straightforward, if not inexpensive, proposition.*

Top Left: *The Ellena, and five wooden boxes of crated parts, arrive safely in Arizona. The trip home was without incident. The new owner didn't really believe he'd bagged the car and that it was now tucked safely in his own trailer. Unloading, inventory, and much parts chasing lay ahead.*
Top Right: *Fortunately, new owner and converted Ferrari treasure hunter Eddie Montini has some experience with Ferraris, and considerable experience restoring show winning muscle cars, so the depth of the job ahead of him isn't a major mystery. Even though the Ellena is rare when compared to Mustang or Camaro production numbers, enough were made so that their equipment and specifications levels are well known. This restoration will be a lot of work but shouldn't contain too many unsolvable mysteries.* **Bottom Left:** *Squint your eyes and you can picture this face looking fabulous again with single headlights, egg-crate grille, integrated foglights, bumpers, and "prancing horse" badging all shiny and back in place once again. Front-end sheet-metal damage appears minimal, although the long-stored body will take a considerable amount of massaging and finish metalworking to look right.*

the silvers offered for the car when new. His best guess is that the interior was originally tan.

And what of the reportedly rebuilt V-12? Not having any firsthand knowledge that it was actually and properly overhauled (other than evidence of some gasket sealer here and there), he's going to tear into it a bit to determine its real state. And if it's not just perfect and factory-new inside, he'll tear it down completely and overhaul it to his standards. This is all part of his plan for a "Pebble Beach–quality ground-up restoration" once he gathers all the parts needed for the job. The result will surely be worth the adventure.

Montini noted that the car had been stripped and disassembled down to its "last nut, bolt, and washer," and no place is that more evident than in the interior. All the gauges and switchgear were removed, much of it ending up in the wooden crates that came with the car, and there's not a shred of wiring to be seen. Fortunately, Montini has the skill and desire to put the car absolutely right and factory fresh once again. Shades of some of the various paint jobs can be seen in this photo.

Chapter 15

1960 Alfa Romeo Giulietta SZ

THE FABERGÉ EGG OF PERFECTLY FORMED, PINT-SIZE ZAGATO-BODIED ALFAS

All photos courtesy of Kirk Gerbracht.

Most of Italy's great design houses and coach-builders have designed and built many great Alfa Romeos. Pininfarina and Touring certainly did, among others, but few did it better and more often than Zagato. Alfa's relationship with Zagato long predates World War II. Among the most memorable and sought after is the tidy, egg-shaped SZ of 1960–1963. Although a street-legal sports car, its specifications and ultra-light weight screamed "GT–class race car" from the word go. The tiny two-seater with the airy glasshouse wore aluminum body panels and Plexiglas windows for lightness.

Power came from the Veloce-spec 1,300-cc Alfa twin-cam four, running twin Weber carbs, and good for 100 hp. Finned aluminum brake drums aided brake cooling and also saved a few pounds over the usual cast-iron drums.

Exterior trim and ornamentation is spare. The Sprint Zagato wears a rounded rump and an endearing face, encompassing a slightly scaled-down version of Alfa's traditional heart-shaped grille. At first glance, the SZ could be confused with Ghia or Pininfarina design, given the slim A- and C-pillars and expansive use of glass that are the defining nuances of those two coachbuilders. Also note that this particular Zagato doesn't have the trademark "double bubble" roofline so common on much of its work on various Ferraris, Maseratis, Alfas, and Fiats.

The beautifully proportioned body is simple, if bordering on plain, and is bereft of scoops and extraneous surface detail. Perhaps its most distinguishing feature is a boneline running about belt high, just below the window line that runs from the front wheelhouse, rearward through the door, and continuing down each rear fender almost to the taillight. The overall shape is round, curvaceous, and elegantly endearing. This car, chassis AR1012600043, was built in late 1960, originally finished in metallic gray with a red interior.

The cabin of this most sporting of 1,300-cc Alfas was also built for speed if not for luxury and comfort. The black dashboard houses a simple three-instrument binnacle, the floor is covered in black rubber matting, and the seats are simple, lightweight, vinyl-covered buckets. According to information provided by auction house Gooding & Company, the car was sold new in early 1961 in Rome to Gianni Bulgari, of the famous jewelry and luxury goods family. Signore Bulgari put the car to work on the racetrack, under his Scuderia Campidoglio banner.

It appears that he raced the car a dozen or more times in the early 1960s, including competing in the

Above: *The non-original red paint job is clearly old and time worn. It wears a variety of battle scars, some perhaps earned in street driving, others likely the result of on-track meet-ups with other cars while in competition. This angle calls attention to the SZ's compact size and low ride height. A little jewel of a car, for sure.*

Facing Page: *The Alfa's trademark heart-shaped grille is front and center where it belongs, with traditional wing-shaped grille openings to either side. Normally singular chromed metal bars would be in each opening, but they've long been removed from this example. The masking tape on the plastic headlight enclosures is not neat, but auction house Gooding & Company's information underscores that it was done way back when, and the car was raced with them like this.*

world-famous Targa Florio enduro in Sicily, and also in the Tour de France Auto. Most of his results in the big races were DNF (did not finish) but he notably notched a first-in-class result in the Italian Coppa Gallenga Hill Climb event on June 18, 1961.

Bulgari sold the car at the completion of the 1962 racing season; it remained in Italy, and still an frequently seen racing competitor, including another attempt at the Targa in 1963. About that time, the car, originally delivered with open headlights, acquired a set of handsome and aerodynamic Plexiglas headlight covers (which were factory updated on later SZs), à la Ferrari 250 GT Spyder California or Jaguar E-Type.

Bulgari also affixed a pair of alloy Amador-Campagnolo wheels to the rear axles of the car, as they are likely lighter than the factory steel rims, and are designed with radial fins to aid brake cooling, although why did he only swap two wheels out instead of all four? While still in Italy, and sometime before its last race there, the SZ was refinished in a deep metallic red.

The rare Alfa remained in Italy through the summer of 1963 until it was sold to new ownership in New York and shipped to the United States. This owner, Lorenzo Garcia, has owned the car since 1964 and kept it in unmolested as-raced condition in New York until it was pulled out of dry storage and sold to Gooding's consignor for resale at the Scottsdale, Arizona, auction in January 2015.

As presented by Gooding, the dusty, spider web–filled machine appears very complete but had not run in some time; it would likely run and drive with a thorough mechanical reconditioning. The paint is faded and shows its full share of knocks, scrapes, and gouges, with a few spots of minor nonstructural corrosion in the alloy body panels. The cabin is complete but shabby, and the Plexiglas headlight bubbles appear to be held in place with some hastily applied masking tape. The North American Racing Team decals on the front fenders are a bit of a mystery, as it is not known that this car was ever owned, imported, or raced by NART's Luigi Chinetti. The chrome grille bars are missing from the front end's horizontal grille openings, likely removed in period racing to improve cooling. This car wore no bumpers from new, and does not currently.

This is one of those cars that could easily be made mechanically sound, cleaned up a bit, and driven exactly

Above Left: *This is a rare car in any condition. Only about 200 Alfa Romeo Giulietta Sprint Zagato coupes were built during the model's brief production run in the early 1960s. Concours-quality examples with great history and provenance can easily run a million dollars, so maybe this one, which brought less than $600,000 at Gooding & Company's January 2015 Scottsdale, Arizona, auction was a bit of a bargain? Yes, it needs some work, but check out its racing history!*
Above Right: *The original 1,300-cc Alfa twin Cammer looks a little grungy, but complete; it should require a straight-forward effort to put it right and get it running. Or, swap in a 1600 for instant horsepower and more go.* **Below:** *The rounded rump is simple, largely free of ornamentation, and never wore rear bumpers. It was a smart call on Zagato's part, foreseeing that most of these cars would be raced, and that any weight-adding bumpers they designed and attached would likely end up on a shop floor anyway. Lots of glass area contributes to superb visibility out of the compact coupe.*

as it is. Or it would be a prime candidate for a full and complete restoration, being a complete original car of high specification with a clear ownership history and legitimate racing provenance.

Gooding & Company's presale estimate was $600,000 to $800,000, and it only missed that mark by a little: hammered and sold at $577,500. Some experts feel that this was a lot of money for a beat-up old Alfa. Others call it a bargain for such a rare (only about 200 built) example in such original condition with known ownership and racing history.

Either way, I call it cool. The word is that is was purchased by a noted Los Angeles area collector, and his intent is to get the car running and mechanically sound, but not to restore it any further. He plans to drive it in the same condition in which it was raced in Italy five decades ago. Sounds like a plan.

Top Left: *Rare and unusual Campagnolo wheels ended up on the rear of this car only; why not four wheels? The radial shape around the rim was designed to aid brake-drum cooling.* **Top Right:** *Several chunks of thick red paint went missing from this car during nearly 60 years of international life. A matter of personal taste here: If I were lucky enough to own this car, I'd return it to its original medium metallic gray finish; it's factory originality versus barn-fresh condition. This battle-scared paint was applied while the car was relatively new and was its race livery.* **Bottom Left:** *Luckily, some of the proof of provenance has survived in the form of these original inspection and entry stickers on the Alfa's windshield; evidence of the SZ's participation in the Targa Florio is particularly valuable. Stickers such as this are often fragile; they can dry up and blow away when a car sits in storage that is too hot or too dry, or are stripped out by an overzealous restorer. Fortunately, that's not the case here.* **Bottom Right:** *A simple cockpit, focused on the business of driving. Three gauges are plenty, and in this case they are focused where they belong: directly in front of the pilot. The interior is the factory color and appears to be original.*

Chapter 16

1961 Aston Martin DB4

GREAT CAR, BAD BARN

All photos courtesy of RM Auctions.

This hapless Aston Martin DB4 is an example of a "barn find done wrong." Not in the finding, and, of course, none of this car's conditional challenges are its fault, but Aston Martin chassis DB4/718/R couldn't have been stored in more damaging conditions (short of the *Titanic*'s cargo hold). A damp, drafty, old barn with a dirt floor and rubbish strewn about is an entirely inappropriate place for a desirable exotic car.

Metaphorically speaking, the DB4 was a huge car for Aston Martin. It was the first all-new design of the David Brown ownership era not stemming directly from existing, immediate post-war, or early 1950s architecture. It was a virtually new chassis and an absolutely new body design, although from the body shape and grille alone, there was no question that it was an Aston. Underhood was an all-new 3.7-liter dual overhead cam straight-6. It finally moved Aston past the old W. O. Bentley–designed 6s that lived under Aston Martin hoods for many years.

The DB4 also was the poster child for a new design relationship with Carrozzeria Touring of Milan, Italy. Touring was known for its superleggera (super light) con-struction method of fitting aluminum body panels over a superstructure of small-diameter welded-steel tubing. Although Touring developed this method, production DB4s were built this way in England, not Italy.

The DB4 spawned many great models, including the shorter wheelbase, special lightweight racing DB4GT. Later came the now rare and highly sought after super-expensive DB4GT Zagato (see Chapter 17). Of course, the car that followed the DB4 in the company's model chronology, the DB5, became famous in the James Bond films.

The DB4 had it all: power, looks, luxury, comfort, brand breeding and hand-built rarity. It was a performer too. In standard trim wearing dual side-draft carbs, the new 3.7-liter straight-6 was good for 240 hp, backed by a 4-speed manual transmission. This may not have sounded all that impressive even for the day, since the competing Jaguar E-Type was rated at 265 hp at the time, and most Chevrolet Corvettes were well over 300.

Although it's fast, the DB4 isn't purely about straight-line speed; it's a luxury grand touring sports car for the deeply-funded and well-dressed gentleman with an equally elegant companion while touring Europe, or perhaps for taking to the Alps during ski season, or for that summer week down in Cannes or Monaco.

In preparation for its Monterey, California, auction in August 2014, RM Auctions shared the DB4's history: "This DB4, chassis number DB4/718/R, was delivered on July 27, 1961, through agent C. Williams, as recorded on the Aston Martin factory build sheet. The same sheet notes that the car was outfitted with Smiths instruments in mph (unusual for a U.K.-delivery car), a heated backlight, two Marchal fog lamps, and a Motorola 818 radio. It was finished in the body color of Snow Shadow Grey over Dark Blue Connolly trim. During its quarter-century in England, the car was registered as 7727 JW.

Above: *This is certainly no way to treat an Aston Martin! The conditions couldn't be worse for preserving a car in storage: dirt floor, uninsulated walls, and trash all about that is great for causing incidental body damage as well as attracting rodents and other animals that wreak havoc on an old car. The opening in this wood barn wall lets in plenty of cold, damp air, rain, and creatures of all sorts. This car's past, present, and future don't look good from any angle, but it's obvious that all of the important glass, light lenses, bezels, and chrome are intact. Note original U.K. license plate.*

Facing Page: *It's a profile any enthusiast will recognize. One of the major differences between this street-version DB4, the DB4-GT, and the later DB5 is that the latter two cars have glassed-in headlights.*

Below: *Having been extracted from less than ideal barn storage, this now blue DB4 looks great with its tires inflated and parked on the street, in the sun where it belongs.*

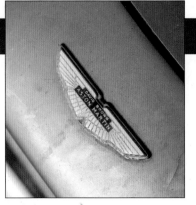  

Left: *The winged "DB" Aston badge denotes a great car with a great engine beneath this bonnet. Even though there were several DB Aston Martins before the DB4, this was the first really all-new chassis architecture that didn't rely on basics from the early 1950s models. It was larger, heavier, faster, and more sophisticated than any previous Aston offering, and it led the way to the DB4GT, DB4GT Zagato, DB5, and the 1960s DB models that followed it.* **Middle:** *The original number and VIN tag sits where it does not belong; it's rusted but readable and in one piece. It appears to have been detached from its normal spot in the engine bay, perhaps to prevent it from being stolen or deteriorating further. The numbers on it do match this car. Note the seriously layered and flaking blue paint.* **Right:** *The mileage appears to be original, and not too much for a 53-plus-year-old British gent of a car. DB4s are tough, robust cars that, when given proper upkeep, can possibly double this mileage before an overhaul is necessary.*

"Interestingly, the 'JW' refers to John Windridge, a senior director of Castrol Limited. Of course, the name Castrol needs no introduction to even the casual vintage racing enthusiast. It is the motor oil that was employed in virtually every European fast touring car of the era, and Aston Martin was no exception. In fact, in 1960, Aston Martin and Castrol had entered into a sponsorship relationship with each other. According to Tony Bonner, a former Castrol chauffeur, the oil company decided that it would be appropriate to keep a DB4 in the company fleet, and so this car was acquired for Windridge by Castrol as an 'executive car.' It was delivered directly to Castrol House, the company's recently completed and strikingly modern headquarters building on Marylebone Road in Westminster, as is documented in factory records.

"Factory service records indicate extensive use of the car in its first few years, with factory maintenance continuing in the ownership of the second caretaker, Ronald Rawden, an active British enthusiast, who, in five decades of connoisseurship, also enjoyed numerous Jaguars, BMWs, and, indeed, other Astons.

"Rawden later recalled, 'I found the DB4 in a garage in Woodford, Essex. It was a thrilling experience driving it home for the first time, not found with many other cars. After many years, the car needed an overhaul, and I decided to do the work mostly myself. I took the engine completely out of the car and stripped it down to the last nut and bolt. I was in constant touch with the service department at Aston Martin in Newport Pagnell, who gave me all the information and spare parts required.' The Aston was registered in his ownership as 1 EXL.

"The factory's last servicing of the car occurred in late 1969 and early 1970, while in the ownership of Mr. Sudbury, of Suffolk, who acquired the car with 21,589 miles on its odometer in September 1969 and commissioned a

Ah, the key is in the ignition; something all too often lost in barn-find situations, and thus a tip to all aspiring barn finders: Once you make the deal for the car, make sure to ask for all spare parts (new or used), books and manuals, keys, license plates, ownership and registration documents, tool rolls, and any other history or records that supports the car's provenance. When inspecting the car, make a note of anything that appears to be missing; all too often, the missing (and rare or expensive) pieces are stored somewhere in the barn, attic, basement, or car parked right next to your find.

 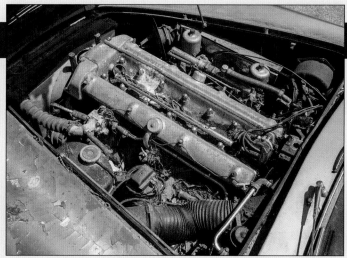

Left: *This is the beginning of the end for most barn finds; but it could be the beginning of the road to redemption. The brooding DB4 was extracted from its musty barn, loaded on the back of a flatbed truck, and then was on its way to auction in California. It was a no-sale the first time around in August 2014.* **Right:** *This may, at first glance, resemble a Jaguar XK straight-6, but instead it is master engine designer Tadek Marek's fabulous Aston Martin 3.7.*

full road inspection and new battery. The last note in the factory records is a handwritten comment indicating the car's acquisition on August 30, 1985, by K. W. Robbins, Esq., of Madrid, Spain.

"It is believed that not long after, the car was escorted to a new home in the United States. It was acquired by a gentleman in Mississippi, in whose ownership it remained hidden from sight before emerging recently as a literal 'barn find.' Today, it presents as the ideal basis for a restoration, with Rawden's work undone by time and age. It still wears its repaint in Caribbean Blue from the 1960s, and while the interior and trim are largely complete, they, along with the rest of the car, require a full restoration. Reportedly, the engine is free, although the car does not presently run and drive."

This amazing find has a well-documented history, and in authentically and correctly restored condition would be worth a considerable amount of money. Its condition suggests that a simple recommissioning wouldn't make the car particularly attractive or roadworthy. A comprehensive restoration is the only sensible path for it to enjoy a viable future as a desirable classic.

What fate awaits it? To date, that is unsure. Despite drawing a high bid of $290,000 at the RM auction event, the car didn't meet the seller's expectations and the bidding was closed as a no-sale.

Left: *"Hurting but complete" describes the interior, and although it's possible that the cabin could be stripped, cleaned, treated, and reinstalled it really deserves a complete redo.* **Right:** *The original deep-blue leather seats are beautifully patinated. It would take considerable deep cleaning and reconditioning to make this cabin as comfortable and luxurious as it was, but a really skilled interior restoration expert could probably save it. This might not be a bad idea because repainting and rechroming this car will cost many tens of thousands of dollars, and reusing this interior will make the proposition of buying and restoring this car much more feasible.*

Chapter 17

1961 Aston Martin DB4GT Zagato

THE CROWN JEWEL IN A ZAGATO AUTOMOBILE COLLECTION

D r. Nicholas Begovich is an interesting and accomplished gentleman. According to a biography published by the California Institute of Technology's alumni association, "Dr. Begovich spent 22 years with Hughes Aircraft, starting in 1948 as a research physicist and becoming a vice president in the late 1950s. He joined Litton Industries in 1970 as a corporate vice president and president of its Data Systems Division. Since 1976, Begovich has been a consultant to the Applied Physics Laboratory of Johns Hopkins University and other organizations. He is a member of the American Physics Society and a Fellow of the Institute of Electrical and Electronic Engineering."

Much of Dr. B's work involved the development of modern, post–World War II radar and radio systems. He also spent considerable time traveling the world, and often bought cars and brought them back to his Southern California home. There were Porsches, a DeTomaso and other Italians, and the very spectacular 1961 Aston Martin DB4GT Zagato chassis DB4GT/10187/L ("L" indicating left-hand-drive).

If you're not familiar with the DB4GTZ, you may really want to invest the time to get to know this car. Simply put, it's one of the world's greatest-ever sports cars. It is, perhaps, the high watermark of Aston Martin's longtime, on again, off again, carbuilding relationship with Italian carrozzeria Zagato of Milan. This very special grand touring coupe was introduced at the 1960 London Motor Show, riding atop a modified Aston Martin DB4GT chassis, wearing terribly curvaceous and sensuous Zagato aluminum coachwork, powered by a hopped-up 3,670-cc version of Aston's torquey and race-proven twin cam straight-6.

The initial plans called for a 25-car run of the Z model, but just 19 were built. Although not specifically conceived as a GT-class racer, many were in fact raced, with some success. Jim Clark notably drove one, although the Zagato DB4 was never quite the competition match of its contemporaries such as the Ferrari 250 SWB coupe and later 250 GTO. It doesn't matter, because it is achingly beautiful, a thrill to drive, rare, and extremely valuable.

By way of full disclosure, I must mention that this car and its amazing story were previously published in Tom Cotter's landmark book, *The Cobra in the Barn,*

A justifiably proud David Sydorick sits comfortably with a large, expensive, limited-edition book about the life and history of the DB4GT Zagato. The page is turned to an "as found" photo of DB4GT/0187/L, still painted red, and missing its entire rear axle and suspension, just as he first saw it parked in Dr. Nicholas Begovich's garage.

published in 2005. Given that I have a long standing personal relationship with the car's owner, and had the chance to inspect the car personally and photograph it expressly for this volume, I elected to include it; this is a significant point because the mention of the car in Cotter's book includes a factually similar description but no photographs, and it's a car so beautiful that it's worth repeating the story to see the pictures.

Deals Require Patience

Like Dr. Begovich, David Sydorick is an interesting and accomplished gentleman, for entirely different reasons than the noted Cal Tech scientist. A man of considerable means and taste, Sydorick owns an outstandingly curated and presented classic car collection. Among his tastes is a deep-seated love of all things Zagato. Thus, he has Zagato-bodied Alfas, Maseratis, and a super-rare Zagato-clothed mid-1950s Ferrari 250 GT Z.

Sydorick is first-name friends with the Zagato family and the company's seminal designer who created the DB4GT Zagato and many other Zagato greats, Ercole Spada. Signore Spada joined Zagato as a young man, and immediately began creating winners on his drawing board, and, more than anyone else, defined the Zagato look.

DB4GT/0187/L represented the model's debut at the Turin motor show in 1961, and was ultimately sold to an Italian customer in 1962. Its original color scheme was Lancia blue exterior paint, with an off-white leather interior. Along the way and throughout the 1960s, it was dolled up a bit and mildly customized for auto show duty, which included a repaint with medium bronze metallic, and much of the exterior trim was replated gold. Handsome? Maybe, or maybe not. Eye-catching? For sure.

The car ultimately made its way into the United States in the late 1960s when Dr. Begovich purchased it. As a scientist of extreme talent, Begovich liked to know how things work, and often felt he could make them work better. He has a habit of buying an exotic car, driving it for a while, and then taking it apart to discover the makeup of its innards with the intent to improve upon the design or componentry. Such was the case with his rare Aston Zagato.

As you'd expect, Dr. B has a well-equipped and organized garage in his Southern California home. Sometime around 1974 he put the Italian-tailored Aston Martin up on jackstands, and removed the rear axle and suspension. And that's as far as he went with it, for several decades.

Very few people knew he even had the car, and fewer still ever saw it. David Sydorick caught wind of it, and wanted it; it's one of the most ultimate expressions of his Zagato thirst. Sometime around 2000 or 2001, he was invited into Begovich's garage. His first instinct was to run to the car, peel back the cover, and envision it as his

Facing Page: *It might be difficult to name a more beautiful, early-1960s sporting gran turismo than David Sydorick's ultimately elegant 1961 Aston Martin DB4GT Zagato, parked in his courtyard. The bust of Michelangelo's David, seen just at the back of the car, appears to be appraising the car in agreement.*

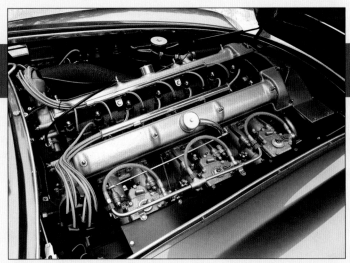 

Left: *The DB4GT's 3.7-liter version of Aston's seminal straight-6 was rated at 314 hp, just a few more horses than the highly spec'd 3.0-liter V-12 Ferrari 250 GTO. Sir Stirling Moss and the late Formula 1 champion Jim Clark raced DB4G-TZs; these cars also competed at the 24 Hours of Le Mans and a variety of GT races around Europe in the early 1960s.* **Right:** *No junk in this trunk, just the required spare wheel and tire, and an oversized aluminum fuel tank.*

own. But being the perceptive and astute man that he is, the "little voice in his head" told him not to do that, and he listened. In fact, for this first visit, he only wanted to establish its existence.

He was right, and when it came up in conversation, he commented, "Well maybe we can talk about that next year." Sydorick and Begovich became friends, often joining each other for the Monterey Car Week and Pebble Beach Concours d'Elegance, where Sydorick is frequently an entrant and class winner.

After a fair amount of ducking and weaving, it became clear to Begovich that Sydorick wanted to buy the car, but that transaction wasn't destined to happen quickly or immediately. Sydorick finally got to peel the cover off his prize, and it was exactly as rumored and reported: all original and very complete, registering low miles on the odometer.

Sydorick recalls, "It was jacked up, with the whole rear axle assembly removed; still sporting the tacky candy red paint, funny seat upholstery, and gold plated wheels and other trim, but it was beautiful."

A high-for-the-time price was negotiated, and Sydorick began funneling piles of money to Begovich, and before long, he'd paid the entire purchase price. Sydorick adds, "Now I didn't in any way distrust that he would ever back out on the deal, but we'd done the whole thing on a handshake, I'd paid for the car, and still didn't have it in my possession."

There really was no need to worry, as Begovich only needed to establish a financial mechanism whereby the sale would benefit his alma mater, Cal Tech. Ultimately, it was accomplished through trusts, grants, donations, and

other paperwork machinations. Sydorick's patience and gentle persistence paid off, yielding the car he wanted so desperately. Everybody won.

Just Listen to the Car

It required some careful planning, balancing, and securing to get the Aston Martin (without its rear axle installed) packed and loaded onto a truck, and then safely transported about an hour away to Sydorick's home. Once there, it was wheeled into his fabulous garage compound for some contemplative study about how to best and most appropriately restore the machine. Sydorick invited a steady parade of knowledgeable car experts, friends, and others to see the car and help him figure out what color to paint it. The non-original metallic red didn't appeal to him in any way, nor did the gold-plated trim. The original Lancia Blue would not have been the wrong choice; it's an elegant hue and the car's birth color.

Sydorick considered several different specialists for the restoration work, ultimately settling on Pennsylvania-based Aston Martin specialist Steel Wings. He was most intrigued, and at the same time most perplexed, by the Zen-like advice given him by noted automotive expert, historian, researcher, and collector Miles Collier. Collier flew from Florida to California to see the car in person, and to consult with Sydorick. His final advice was, "David, just listen to the car, it'll tell you what color it has to be."

Sydorick listened hard, and the answer was an iconic, not too dark, not too light, shade of metallic green that would likely look great on almost any car, but is

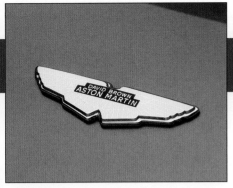  

Left: *Despite its Italian body design and construction, the DB4GTZ is nothing but pure Aston Martin, and some suggest that it is the very highest watermark of the marque's long and storied history. It is only slightly lighter and smaller, and yet it's sportier than the DB4GT architecture upon which it is based.* **Middle:** *The mark of, not Zorro, but Zagato of Milan. Ercole Spada crafted its sensuous bodywork from handcrafted aluminum. Just 19 of the original DB4GTZs were built, and today they're worth many millions of dollars each.* **Right:** *The 16-inch rolling stock on knock-off wire wheels suit this special Aston Martin's sporting purpose and image perfectly. It would be difficult to imagine its perfect period looks and persona riding on alloy wheels.*

particularly appealing on an Aston Martin. So those were his marching orders to Steel Wings, and the car was disassembled down to its last nut and grommet, restored to the very highest levels of concours quality and originality, with particular attention paid to sorting it out to be driven, and not just shown.

It's a winner in both categories, and its happy new owner drives it often and with great enthusiasm. It has also been shown and won big at the world's most significant concours, including a best-of-show win at the Concorso d'Eleganza Villa d'Este in Italy, as well as a class and special awards winner at the Pebble Beach Concours d'Elegance. Steel Wings' work has held up remarkably; the restoration is now a decade old and the car looks as new and minty fresh as the day it was completed. This is a signifi-

cant point because the car has been driven considerably, and shipped all over the world for various meetings and concours events, and transportation is seldom easy on a show-level automobile.

Sydorick takes great and legitimate pride in this fabulous, elegant, and historic machine, and particularly enjoys some of the comments he's heard about it from onlookers. One in particular was heard at an important concours, "It's a very well-mannered car . . . with a hot body." He recalls unloading the car at another show in Connecticut on a foggy morning when the car's voluptuous shapes were further softened by the swirling gray mist, and one onlooker commented to David that, "I'll bet you never say no to her."

Who could?

65°

THIS IS THE MONTEREY PENINSULA

The Sorrentino/Begovich/Sydorick DB4GTZ takes pride of place at Pebble Beach during that show's very special recognition of Zagato coachwork and an important Aston Martin anniversary. (Photo courtesy of David Sydorick Collection)

Chapter 18

A Tale of Two Lussos

HOW STRANGE THAT TWO NEARLY IDENTICAL AND FABULOUS FERRARIS END UP IN BARN-FIND CONDITION

All photos courtesy RM Auctions and Matt Stone.

The late Chuck Jordan, a former vice president of design at General Motors and a man of considerable taste and design sense, as well as being a Ferrari owner and expert, once told me that, "the Lusso is the most elegant Ferrari ever created." Not the fastest, not the most flamboyant, not the rarest, or most exciting, but the most elegant. And he makes a strong point.

Produced for the 1963 and 1964 model years only, the Lusso is a fabulous two-seat-only coupe built on Ferrari's 2,400-mm (94.5-inch) wheelbase front-engine gran turismo chassis. It has long, lean bodylines, a slim roof, and slim window pillars; it is devoid of overly racy-looking body details such as wings, spoilers, vents, gills, and grilles. The clean and perfectly proportioned coachwork is the design of Pininfarina, of course. It was rendered in a combination of steel and aluminum; it wore a full, wraparound rear bumper and a smaller front bumper with small chrome bumperettes at the lower leading edge of each front fender. Even though the car's racy rear windowline gave the impression of having a hatchback or liftback, there was no such thing; the trunk (or boot) has its own proper lid, and the rear window glass is fixed in place. The comfortable two-seat-only cabin was fully trimmed in fine leather.

Power for this model comes from the seminal 3.0-liter Ferrari Colombo single overhead cam V-12 rated at 240 hp, backed by a 4-speed manual transmission.

"Lusso" translates roughly as "luxury," and it was often referred to as the GTL: gran turismo lusso. It was never intended to be a racing model although some were raced with reasonable success. Moneyed enthusiasts, contemporary hipsters, and style mavens bought them new, including Steve McQueen and Eric Clapton.

Although the odd Lusso has been chopped into convertible (Spyder) form, Ferrari officially offered the Lusso only as a coupe. Depending on whose numbers you believe, 350 or 351 Lussos were built over an 18-month period in 1963–1964. They have always been prized and valuable, but have today risen to a very high level of desirability in the Pantheon of "Enzo era" V-12 Ferrari gran turismos.

It would seem reasonable to assume that, given this car's desirability and rank as a blue chip collectible car, every existing Lusso would be in perfectly maintained or restored condition. However, as evidenced by these two remarkable examples that were sold at auction in 2014, I've learned that even great cars fall on hard times.

The red example shown here is chassis number 5233 GT, and the sinewy black Lusso is chassis 5249 GT. It's intersting that they are just 16 chassis numbers apart, both listed as 1964 models, and could have very well been under construction in the Carrozzeria Scaglietti body plant in Modena, Italy, at the same time.

The 5233 was originally silver and sold new through Ferrari's dealer in Rome in late 1963. The purchaser was a businessman, who ultimately took the car home to Karachi, Pakistan. It remained in his and his family's ownership for the following five decades.

Above: *Regardless of the color, the rake and profile of a 250 GT Lusso is unmistakable, and handsome in any surrounding. The 5249 GT was painted black from birth, and still looks great in this classic hue, particularly with its factory red and black interior.*

Facing Page: *Faded non-original paint and grungy trim notwithstanding, Ferrari Lusso 5233 GT cuts a dashing figure sitting straight and level on its original Borrani wire wheels. The owner added the fender decals somewhere along the way, and this car remained in single-family ownership in Karachi, Pakistan, from the day it was sold new in 1963 until the summer of 2014.*

Along the way, it was repainted Rosso Corsa (racing red), with yellow and black Cavallino Rampante stickers pasted to the fenders. Do not confuse these stickers with the similar looking enameled metal badges installed at great additional cost by the factory on current Ferraris.

Obviously the car's life in Pakistan wasn't one of pampered storage and constant attention. Its non-original paint is faded and chalky, its interior is dry and torn, its chrome is rusted, and its aluminum alloy trim is tarnished. As such, it's a perfect example for a platinum-level restoration since it appears to have never suffered any accident damage. Recent verification shows that it still contains its original engine, transmission, and rear axle

Left: *A big round taillight and a dual-outlet ANSA exhaust; it couldn't be anything but a Ferrari. The small badge next to the license plate indicates that this New York owner belonged to the Ferrari Club of America.* **Middle:** *Old registration tags are great evidence of where a car has lived. They also can often tell you the most recent time it was licensed for road use. In this case it looks like the answers are New York, and some time in the mid-1970s.* **Right:** *As on the red car, the Borrani wheels are a bit grungy. They will be straightforward to restore and once again be safe and look like new.*

Left: *This complete, proper, and original Lusso-spec Colombo 3.0-liter Ferrari V-12 is also numbers matching to the original build data. These engines are sweet runners with lots of revvy power and an unmatchable sound as it winds through the gears.* **Right:** *Here's a fun fact you may not know about the twin oil filters on Ferrari's Colombo 3.0-liter V-12. One of them is for looks and symmetry only. It's a real filter that screws into the engine's aluminum front-cover casting properly, but it isn't plumbed and filters no oil. Which is it? It's the one on the passenger's side.*

of proper specification; it's a matching numbers example. The odometer reads just 26,000 kilometers (approximately 16,000 miles), certainly low original miles for a 50-year-old exotic machine. Not as pretty as it once was, but with the right stuff it can be fabulous once again.

Upon completion in late 1963, Lusso 5249 GT was painted black in production, imported by Luigi Chinetti to the United States, and sold new to a New York enthusiast. It appears that it lived its entire life in that state; many photographs of it show the Manhattan skyline in the background. The red interior is also factory installed. From a mechanical and equipment standpoint, it appears to have been configured in virtually identical trim to that

of the Lusso 5233 GT, except for the differences in color combination.

It spent more than a decade in regular use and was last licensed for road use in New York in 1976. Despite the appearance of some hasty, minor paint touch ups here and there, the car is certified as having never been restored, shown, or offered for public sale prior to August 2014.

Like the red car from Pakistan, it has suffered the minor scarring and degradation resulting from long-term storage that was definitely not museum quality, but is nonetheless remarkably complete and original. And as with the red car, it could be tidied up a bit, mechanically recommissioned, and driven in its current condition. However, given its originality, completeness, and superb factory color combination, it's a prime example ripe for a complete, concours-quality restoration.

At what prices come all this history, speed, elegance, dust, and a little surface rust? RM Auctions sold the red Lusso 5233 GT at its Monterey, California, sale on August 15, 2014, for $1,980,000 including fees and commissions. Gooding & Company auctioneers sold the black Lusso 5249 GT at its Pebble Beach, California, sale, also in August 2014, for $2,365,000 including fees and commissions.

The Lusso's clean look is remarkably devoid of trim, with only a small hood scoop indicating that some serious horses lie beneath. Note how handsomely the extra pair of foglights have been designed to be a part of and recessed into the handsome front fascia.

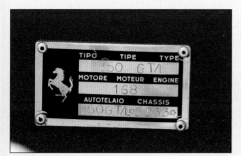

Left: *It's all numbers-matching for 5233, as documented by a check of all of the powertrain components and comparison with the original data tag, which is in good condition still in its proper location.* **Middle:** *The hood scoop is tapered and tame compared to that of many Ferraris, particularly the aggressive race-only models. Yet it's enough to draw in a little cool air to help feed the V-12's three Weber carbs.* **Right:** *The trademark Ferrari egg-crate grille wears the chrome prancing horse badge; these details are right on any Ferrari, no matter how racy or luxurious their missions in life. This grille appears undamaged, but will take a considerable amount of cleaning and careful polishing to make look concours-ready again.*

Above Left: *The ravages of time and storage have, well, ravaged 5233's interior. The leather is dry, hard, and torn and will require complete restoration to be beautiful again. The original materials exist as a perfect pattern and color sample for whoever tackles that project.* **Above Right:** *Among the Lusso model's more interesting design cues is the instrument panel layout. The ancillary gauges (temp, charging, fuel level, etc.) are placed front and center to the driver. The speedo and tach are placed more in the middle of the dash; although canted toward the driver, they are also visible to the passenger. This car's interior appears to have fared somewhat better than 5233, although it is also tired and musty. It's likely that this one has a much better chance of being thoroughly reconditioned and perhaps saved and reused. It's also possible that this car may have spent some time on the racetrack or at time trials given the installation of competition-style seat-belt harnesses. However, such activity is not confirmed in the car's auction catalog description.* **Below:** *This is the profile that caused many experts and designers to list the Lusso among the most elegant Ferrari designs of all time. Pininfarina designs have long been lauded for their trim window and roof pillar designs, airy greenhouses, and perfectly balanced proportions. The long hood and short rear deck keep the shapes moving forward, with the power balanced over the rear wheels.*

Chapter 19

1963 Iso Rivolta IR 300 GT

AS KERMIT SAID, "IT'S NOT EASY BEING GREEN."

All photo by Boris Adolf ©2014, courtesy of RM Auctions.

The Rivolta family of Milan, Italy, made its industrial fortune during the 1950s and 1960s, primarily from the production of refrigeration equipment. Family patron Renzo and son Piero, as you might expect, indulged themselves in high-performance automobiles. At some point, Renzo decided he was capable of building a better line of elegant gran turismos than his friendly rivals Ferrari and Lamborghini. He went to the world's best Italian coachbuilders for his body designs, as did many other low-volume automobile producers of the day. He also decided that there was no reason to attempt to design and build his own engines.

So, like Intermechannica, deTomaso, England's Bristol, and many others, he looked to the smooth, powerful, reliable, and inexpensive V-8 engines produced in the United States. Rivolta established a mechanism to purchase the powertrains that had proven to be so successful in America's only real sports car at the dawn of the 1960s, the Chevrolet Corvette. Indeed, the venerable small-block Chevy V-8 had the right stuff for the Rivolta's planned line of gran turismos.

It made sense. The engine was produced in large quantity, in a wide variety of power ratings, and could be backed by a 4-speed manual or an automatic transmission. Chevy V-8s were available in plentiful supply and were anything but temperamental. In the name of cost management, they were affordable for the Rivoltas to buy.

The first fruit of their labors was the Iso Rivolta. The young Giorgetto Giugiaro, who was already making a name for himself at Bertone, designed this handsome and elegant 2+2. Although other cars were built with higher compression, higher output 327-ci engines, most Rivoltas carried the 5.3-liter 300-hp rendition of the venerable Corvette 327, backed by a 4-speed BorgWarner manual transmission.

The cars were beautifully built and luxuriously trimmed, with sumptuous leather interiors highlighted by genuine wood trim, full instrumentation, and other upmarket touches such as power windows and air conditioning. When production began for the 1962 model year, the intent was to sell the car into a wide variety of the world's car markets. This made the IR 300 GT an ideal competitor to Ferrari's mid-size 2+2, the 250 GTE. Even though a V-12 engine powered the 250 GTE, its power output closely matched the Iso's; both proved to be superlative high-speed luxury grand tourers and were popular among the jet set of the day. The Rivolta was the first of several Iso models that the company produced during the 1960s and early 1970s; they sold approximately 800 units during the model's seven-year run.

The Iso Rivolta has become a sought-after collector car, and prime examples sell for strong money. This of course, begs the question, how did the forlorn green example pictured here fall into such shabby, although highly complete, condition?

According to RM Auctions, which consigned the car for sale at its prestigious Monaco 2014 sale: "Chas-

Above: *The Rivolta's front visage is clean and generally unadorned. Its simple crossbar grille and horseshoe shaped grille badge separates it clearly from its Ferrari, Lamborghini, and Maserati competitors of the day.*

Facing Page: *As is typical of most Giugiaro designs, the Rivolta is well balanced and well proportioned. The greenhouse is airy, the window pillars are relatively slim, and the Rivolta GT looks elegant and properly Italian on its Borrani wire wheels. The rear overhang is rather long; this provides a modicum of rear-seat legroom for the "+2" passengers, and to make for respectable trunk/cargo capacity.*

sis IR 330058, in March 1964, was delivered new to Andreas Gut of Switzerland, who drove it in Zurich for 13 years. In November 1977, with only 11,530 kilometers believed to have been recorded, Gut put his Rivolta into dry storage. It remained hidden away for 37 years, and it has only recently emerged as a new 'discovery.' It's a wonderful early-production Rivolta that has its original matching-numbers engine, chassis, and body."

Gut certainly exhibited excellent taste in selecting such a fine automobile to begin with, but it appears to be the victim of some very questionable modifications along the way. RM submits that the faded metallic green paint and the russet brown leather interior are the car's original. Although the car doesn't appear

Left: *Luckily, all of the car's chrome trim and switchgear is still in place. Replacing this stuff drives restorers and owners a little crazy, and quickly drives up the cost.* **Middle:** *This neat chrome hood scoop isn't hiding any notable ram air intake system. Instead, it's just washing a little cool air over the engine's air filter housing.* **Right:** *Exhaust vents in the C-pillar help vent air out of the cabin, and these seem to be in pretty decent condition.*

Left: *This Iso's wood dash and instrument panel are in great condition, which will aid the restoration, preserve original-ity, and save the new owner some money. Let's hope that the next owner does away with the "woolly mammoth" seat covers and restores the proper, russet colored leather seats.* **Right:** *This shot gives you an idea of the original colors of the interior carpeting and leather. It'll be worth restoring this car to factory spec and condition.*

Above Left: *All of the car's VIN and production information plates are properly in place and the bulkheads and engine compartment panels are tidy and rust free.* **Above Right:** *The stainless scuff plates are clean and with no rot; some polishing and fettling will make them look great. Good luck finding a replacement set if these were damaged or missing.* **Below:** *This three-quarter-rear view shows the odd exhaust system mods. The driver-side bank appears intact, even if it is wearing a slightly funky, non-original twin exhaust tip. The passenger-side pipes have gone missing, and are replaced by a single "sidepipe" bolted to the rocker panel. None of this will survive any sort of quality restoration.*

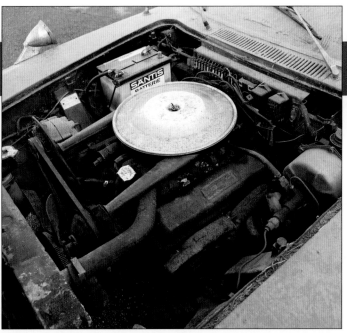

Left: *A 300-horse 327 is often found in many early-1960s Corvettes. The powerplants were sold to Iso by General Motors and came complete with air-cleaner housing, alternator, and most of the other accessories identical to those on the Corvette.* **Top Right:** *This is low mileage for a 50-plus-year-old machine; 11,530 kilometers equals approximately 7,000 miles. The rare Nardi polished aluminum steering wheel is in good condition; it's one of many components supporting the low-mileage claim.* **Bottom Right:** *The Rivolta's trunk is relatively large and usably configured, although this one needs retrimming. The floor appears solid and rust free.*

to have suffered any major accident damage, a few rust bubbles are popping up here and there, perhaps the victim of a long life in Switzerland's harsh winter weather. The exterior chrome is tarnished, pitted, and rusted a little, but all of the hard to replace trim pieces appear to be present.

Gut must have had a taste for stickers, and several unidentified parking, registration, and other types on the window glass. The "CH" decal on the rear fascia denotes Confoederatio Helvetica, or Switzerland, and the car also wears a large faded "GT" decal, made of reflective material, just below its rear bumper.

The most curious "modification" is to the exhaust system. The driver-side pipes appear intact, while the passenger-side bank of exhaust piping clearly fell apart or off, and was replaced by a single chrome "sidepipe" mounted just below the passenger door.

RM summarized its auction catalog description as follows: "The car is ideal for restoration, as it retains its original finishes and is rust-free throughout. The body is in particularly straight and fine condition, and much of the glass, once cleaned, remains clear. The interior will require restoration, but it is wonderfully complete, with lovingly worn russet-brown leather upholstery that could be usable for patterns and its fully instrumented dashboard's gauges still intact.

"The owner reports that the car has 11,530 kilometers, all accumulated prior to its 1977 storage, and that the engine is free and turns easily. This complete and beautifully preserved Rivolta is ready for restoration and to begin life anew on the Riviera."

The car sold in Monaco on Saturday, May 10, 2014, for €22,400, or approximately $31,478 at the then-current exchange rates.

Even though this Rivolta doesn't appear to have any major structural rot in its floor pans, trunk, or rockers, a few rust bubbles are brewing just behind the headlight bezels.

Chapter 20

1964 Shelby Cobra 289

DON'T TOUCH THIS BARN-FRESH, UNRESTORED COBRA; YOU MIGHT RUB OFF SOME OF THE DIRT

Paint that's deep and wet-looking enough to swim in? Pass. Triple chrome plating, polished to a mirrorlike brilliance? Yawn. Glove-soft leather, museum-quality wood trim, and an engine compartment cleaner than most hospital operating rooms? Out, Out, *Out!* Automotive restoration techniques and standards have risen to stratospheric levels. And why not? A picture-perfect machine that sparkles like the display cases at Tiffany's is a great source of pride and stands to win big at the Snootville Concours d'Elegance.

Although performing this sort of resto work demands great skill from teams of talented craftsmen, having it is no more difficult than pillaging your retirement fund. Because there are dozens of shops that can turn out ostensibly perfect "100-point" cars, what's the newest haute couture sought by the world's most in-the-know enthusiasts? Originality. Not the kind that's restored in, but the kind that every car was born with. Something can be refurbished one or 100 times and may be all the more beautiful for it. But it's factory original only once.

If there's anyone besides Carroll Shelby who could rightly wear the nickname "Mr. Cobra," it's Lynn Park. This affable, retired elevator company executive has been into Cobras for more than three decades, yet is as enthusiastic about them as ever. He currently owns 10 of them, but the count has been as high as 13. And how many has he possessed over time? "27. Or 28. No, 27. I think. Yup, 27." Park isn't feigning modesty. He just doesn't dwell on such things. I've seen several of his cars, and they're all in spectacular condition. Then there's Shelby Cobra chassis number 2307.

Fred Offenhauser of the racing engine and speed parts family bought it new in Southern California. "He didn't buy it until 1968 or 1969," Park recalls, "I think the dealer must've used it as a demo and then kept it to drive for a few years. Offenhauser repainted the car immediately. (I guess he just didn't want a red one.) And he drove it until 1975, then parked it. Outside. Under a tarp."

Although Offenhauser was done with the now pale-yellow Shelby, the car wasn't for sale. People in the neighborhood, car collectors, and ardent Cobra fans pursued it for decades, "But Fred's wife chased them away, occasionally with a shotgun. It wasn't until a buddy of mine from Palo Alto heard about the car and went down there with a trailer and bought it. That was about ten years ago."

On his way home, Park's pal stopped to show him what he'd bought. "He said, 'Lynn, I'm going to make this into a race car.'

These are period-correct Cobra seats, old and wonderfully worn, but less torn up than the ones the car came with. Threadbare carpets, and all of the other interior fittings are stock and original to this car. The competition-style belts indicate that this car has assuredly put in a few laps around one racetrack or another.

"I said, 'No, you can't. You cannot do that to this.'

"So, we found him a race car, did some horse trading, and I ended up with this one. As he never took title to it and only had it long enough to sell it to me, I consider myself the second owner."

Park's first inclination was to restore the crusty Cobra to authentic and, of course, showroom condition. "But after I had it a few months and started playing with it, I decided I had to keep it the way it was. People were making such a fuss over it; I had to leave it alone." The disinterment process was straightforward, although it required patience. Park believes that cars were meant to be driven, and he didn't want to do anything to take away from this Cobra's time-warp look. "The best cars you have are the ones that have never been apart. Good or bad, you know what it is."

The amazing Shelby Cobra on these pages is one such automobile. Its dull, pockmarked, timeworn look has even earned it an affectionate nickname: Dirtbag.

"I swapped the seats for another set that were worn but period-correct because the originals were thrashed. I changed the water pump, rebuilt the carb, replaced the fan belt and all the fluids, and then fixed up the exhaust system, although I've never been into the engine. That was a gamble, because it had been sitting so long. Marvel Mystery Oil to the rescue!

"When I first got it running, it smoked a lot. The more I drove it, the less it smoked. Now, it doesn't smoke at all, which is kinda' disappointing; a car that looks like this almost wants to smoke a little. The brake and clutch pedals were frozen; you couldn't move them with both feet. I have hundreds of hours in the preservation of it, because I tried to do it all without changing the look of things or removing any dirt."

Park still appreciates a beautifully presented machine, Cobra and otherwise. Yet he knows he has something different and special. "People flock to this car. When I

Left: *Several decades of license registration tags tells where the car was built, sold, lived under a tarp, and now thrives in Lynn Park's steady-handed and expert care.* **Middle:** *In spite of its dingy demeanor, the factory Cobra-spec Ford 289 Hi-Po fires instantly and runs smoothly. Having driven this car, I can tell you it's a blast to drive (or ride in) and still fast by any measure.* **Right:** *Bumpers, overriders, taillights, and chrome "pencil tip" exhausts are absolutely right and original on this car. And don't look for them to be cleaned up or replated any time soon. Or ever.*

Facing Page: *Lynn Park's very special barn-find Cobra looks little different from when his friend discovered it in Mr. and Mrs. Fred Offenhauser's back yard, and peeled away the rotted tarp covering it. It's now a great runner, and has found an infinitely better home in Park's outstanding, and astounding, "snake pit."*

first got it, it was on display at the Petersen Automotive Museum among more than 100 other Cobras. And it's been on the grass at Pebble Beach. Carroll Shelby himself could not get over this car. He was all over it. Just loved it. You'd be amazed how many people have come to look at it when they're restoring their own. It's become a restoration pattern. It's just the kinda' thing where you say, 'Wait a minute; maybe I shouldn't touch this.'

"There are more and more people thinking that same way."

Like a 911 or XK120, an early Cobra screams sports car. Short, windowless doors provide access to a cockpit that's elegant in its simplicity. A wood-rimmed, alloy, three-spoked steering wheel frames the two most important Stewart Warner instruments. Half a dozen ancillary gauges sit just to the right of the speedo and tach, arranged like so many bowling pins on the instrument panel. The bucket seatbacks come up to your shoulder blades, and the shifter that connects you and the BorgWarner T-10 4-speed transmission is little taller than a Magic Marker.

Park's car is equipped with several factory options, such as Plexiglas sun visors, wind wings, and a Cobra-specific AM radio that proudly declares that it is "All Transistor." The odometer reads fewer than 38,000 miles, and 2307's leather seats wear the creases of a wise old man's face. The black carpeting is faded and threadbare in more than a few places. At least two of the gauges don't work, the dash covering is pulling away here and there, and the vinyl on the rear tonneau cover has had more stitches than most NFL linemen. But like your favorite pair of jeans, broken-in penny loafers, and a well-tailored if slightly worn tweed blazer, it feels so damn comfortable. Breathe in. Yes . . . good old-car smells.

For all the hoo-ha over the more powerful and better-developed 427 Cobras, the earlier, narrower 260- and 289-ci Ford V-8 cars are the ones that gave birth to the legend. They won all the big races, begat the FIA championship-winning Daytona Cobra Coupes, and broke the hearts of Corvette and E-Type owners throughout the mid-1960s. The first-generation Cobra's shapes are less bloated than the big-block model's, its mood is sportier if not as aggressive, and those knock-off wire wheels and rear-exit exhausts are classic 1960s sports car touches.

Wring it Out!

This car and its amazing story of lost and found was previously referenced in Tom Cotter's fine book, *The Cobra in the Barn* ten years ago. However, because the owner is a neighbor and friend of mine, I had the opportunity to photograph it for this book, *and* I had the chance to get behind the wheel and wring the little Cobra about a bit. I feel that this added enough to the story that it was too good of an opportunity to pass up telling it again, albeit from a personal perspective.

Cobra 2307 spews patina from every pore. There's a brief belch of blue smoke as the small-block Ford fires, then it settles into an easy idle with its adjustable lifters rattling softly. It doesn't sound much different from a 1966 Mustang with worn-out glasspack mufflers. The brake pedal is firm, the clutch direct, and the shifter engages first gear with ease. In this world of computer-controlled, electronically enhanced, variable-ratio power-steering systems, it's easy to forget how direct and organic unencumbered steering feels in a car that's light enough not to require any of that stuff. Goose the gas pedal, feel (there's that word again) the clutch take up, and you're away.

Although 271 hp doesn't sound like a lot, in a roadster that weighs little more than 2,000 pounds, it's plenty. Road tests of the day claim a 0-to-60 time

Park knows how lucky he is to have assembled a pack of Cobras, and his passel of other great cars, including a fine Willys coupe, an appropriately Ford-engined 1932 Ford hot rod, some drag racers, and a small variety of other great rides. His garage complex is really its own Cobra museum of sorts, although it's not open to the public in that sense. The photos, posters, parts on the wall and general ephemera complement the great cars within, as well as Park's home office and an arcade's worth of vintage pinball machines.

Left: *Remnants of two factory stickers from 1964 show in the rusty and pitted original air cleaner housing. One gave the air filter specs and part number, the other announced than this engine, is in fact, a "289 Hi-Po." This housing is nearly identical to those atop the proper Shelby-spec Holley four-barrel carb used on 1965-1966 Mustang GTs and many Shelby Mustangs.* **Middle:** *CSX2307 wears several rare factory options, including this very humble AM radio, as well as Plexiglas sun visors and windwings.* **Right:** *The instrument panel and alloy/wood steering wheel scream originality. All the gauges are the proper Stewart Warners, and the 37,862 miles are, of course, original. Park and Carroll Shelby were long-time good friends, and Park credits Carroll with encouraging him to recommission only, and never restore the car to pristine newness.*

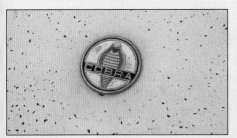

Left: *Original, and seriously valuable, all the Shelby Cobra badging is intact, even if much of the original paint has worn off. Replica Cobra builders would pay huge bucks for a supply of OEM jewelry such as this for their inventory.* **Middle:** *The original grille and grille bars show the pitting of time and outdoor storage. California black and gold plates are period correct and original to this car. Note the old-style pre-area code phone number "Parkview 21010" Unfortunately, you can't dial this number today and buy a new 1964 Shelby Cobra for $6,000.* **Right:** *Park's Cobra barn wears several double-size doors, and double-deep in tandem. Because Cobras are relatively small cars he can really pack them in. Both shop and garage are tidy and immaculate, without being overdressed.*

of about 5.8 seconds, and I wouldn't doubt it. There's ample torque down low, and the real sweet spot begins at about 2,500 rpm. Don't push this unopened 289 much past 5,000 revs, although they were good to 6,500. Hard on the throttle, and the pipes blare a familiar V-8 warble. Downshift and let the engine do the braking, and it burbles and pops as it should. Wonder if there are any tunnels around here.

The shorty shifter makes rowing the trans a joy; love that little T-handle for engaging reverse. Like most of the rest of this car, the clutch and transmission are untouched since they were installed more than 40 years ago. Considering that the chassis design dates back to the AC Ace of the 1950s and there are transverse leaf springs front and rear, the ride quality is good, until the pavement gets choppy. Carroll Shelby said, "The chassis flex

in the early Cobra is part of the suspension. People try to stiffen them up, which kills the handling and the ride."

Cornering the car along the famed Angeles Crest Highway, it hits me. Because I'm not concerned about rock chips, water, or a dirty road surface that would soil the average trailer queen, I relax. I take in the trees, hills, fresh air, and a dazzling orange sunset. I focus more on driving this Cobra than any fear of hurting it. People point and wave. My cheeks hurt. From smiling.

Will Dirtbag ever be for sale? Lynn Park reflects: "I get a lot of questions about that. The first thing people want to know is if it's 'a real Cobra,' which is funny because, obviously, it is. Then they want to know if I want to sell it. And I say, 'No.' Then they want to know when I'm going to start the restoration. And I say, 'Never.' Because this one's done."

Chapter 21

1964 Lamborghini 350 GT

WHEN IS A GT350 NOT A SHELBY MUSTANG? SIMPLE: WHEN IT'S A 350 GT, MAKING IT A LAMBORGHINI

All photos courtesy of Paul Roesler.

The 350 GT was Lamborghini's first production model; it was inspired by the Lamborghini 350 GTV concept car. While many of its design details were substantially modified or updated for production form, the primary footprint and premise of the dazzling concept remained, as did its bespoke Lamborghini 3.5-liter V-12. The 350 GT put Ferruccio Lamborghini on the map as one of Italy's true producers of high-performance exotic cars. They were assembled in the company's own purpose-built factory in Sant A'gata Bolognese, just north of Modena and Maranello, homes of Maserati and Ferrari, respectively.

Lamborghini 350 GT chassis 0102, built originally as a European-spec, two-seat, left-hand-drive example, has led a most interesting, and occasionally troubled international life. Wearing proper Carrozzeria Touring coachwork, it was constructed during the summer of 1964 and is documented as the second production-spec 350 GT built and the first one sold into its retail sales dealer in Geneva. It is also documented as the very car photographed for Lamborghini's 350 GT sales brochure. It seems to have lived much of the 1960s in Europe, changing hands several times during the latter half of the decade.

Sometime in the early 1970s, it was shipped to and sold in the United States. The car was living in New York when, sometime in 1974–1975, at the hands of that owner, it was involved in an accident that seriously damaged the front-end sheet metal, fortunately without doing major or irreparable frame damage. In 1976 it was considered totaled, and the remains were sold off, essentially as spare parts, to someone in Southern California. The car was then put into long-term dry storage, and it sat for a couple of decades.

A Bumpy Journey Home

San Francisco–area enthusiast Paul Roesler entered the picture in 1997. Roesler learned of the car through the well-known longtime classic car enthusiast and dealer Joseph Alphabet. After some negotiations, a deal was struck, which Roesler notes was about double the price for a restored similar example without the accident damage. A deposit was advanced, with final payment and delivery pending.

Above: *Even post-accident, and after all of its years in storage, the car looked pretty good from the back. The split rear bumpers are misaligned, and the taillights and exhaust system have already been removed, but the back end of the car needed no major work. The door's shut lines are still straight, although the same cannot be said of the trunk panel.*

Facing Page: *Perfect once again, resplendent in its original silver over Bordeaux (dark red) with absolutely no hint or indication of its past life as an insurance write-off. Panel alignment is perfect, and the result is a sure show winner, as evidenced by the ribbon on the hood.*

Below: *I never become tired of this look; it's the original inspiration and definition of Lamborghini, before the notions of mid-engine exotics including the future Countach and Aventador. As you'd expect, it was an expensive car when new at about $14,000, and was competitive with grand touring Ferrari 250 GT coupes and similar Maseratis of the mid-1960s.*

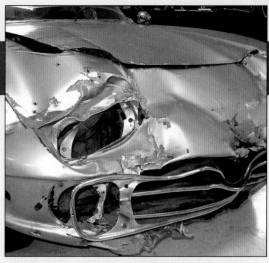

Left: *Ouch! An early 1970s accident punched the 350 GT hard in the nose, and in spite of no significant frame damage, it was considered totaled, which seems unthinkable today. At the time, the car was a ten-year-old used sports car; its future collectibility and price appreciation weren't even a thought. The car was sold for scrap and parts, yet luckily it was never parted out. Instead, it was parked inside for long-term storage with an unknown future.* **Right:** *Aluminum is fairly malleable and can often be reshaped if the mangling isn't too bad; in this case a major nose replacement job was needed. Some of the metal was replaced while some of it was reformed into shape. Owner Roesler freely credits Symbolic Motor Cars and lead technician Bill Attaway for a masterful job of saving the car.*

About this time, a third party (who must remain nameless) attempted to buy the car and ship it back to Europe. Alphabet, still representing the seller, discussed the turn of events with Roesler. Concerned with losing not only his deposit, but also his chance to own the car, Roesler was now completely psychologically invested in the rare Lambo, and wanted it badly.

The rest of the story would make a good reality television show segment or movie. Fortunately, Alphabet intended to make good on his commitment to Roesler after verifying that the deposit he received really came from Roesler. Because the mysterious third party's offer came with time limitations, the seller told Roesler that he needed to complete the deal the following day: Pay the entire balance in cash and pick up the car immediately.

Obviously, Roesler had work to do. He contacted a vehicle transport company; he needed a driver and an enclosed transport truck in Southern California the next day for a one-way run to the Bay Area with a single car aboard. He offered to pay double the normal rate just to

Left: *Even though the wreck didn't substantially damage or bend the tubular steel chassis, the hit was hard enough to wrinkle and tear the front fenders and spring the hood. Symbolic worked hard to save as much of the factory-original Carrozzeria Touring coachwork as possible, replacing only what was absolutely necessary.* **Middle:** *The rear fenders also show the effects of time on the paint and chrome. It's likely that because the car was considered a total loss, it wasn't treated gently during moving or storage. Fortunately, few of the irreplaceable hand-crafted parts were missing when the car was torn down for restoration.* **Right:** *Although aluminum panels don't rust, it's clear that moisture worked its way underneath the paint here, bubbling the original silver and corroding the Carrozzeria Touring badgework. Lamborghini's new Sant'A'gata assembly factory didn't have stamping capability at the time, so the panelwork was done at Touring in nearby Milan.*

Left: *The rear trunk area had also suffered during the car's long-term storage; it looked shabby and had a layer of surface rust. Remember, this car, being such an early example, was virtually hand built. The giant dunk tanks of corrosion-proofing paint into which today's car bodies are dipped prior to assembly did not exist in Italy back then. The metal was lucky to receive some primer and a thin coat of "chassis black" paint.* **Right:** *Now that's better. Much of the nose was rebuilt using fresh aluminum sheeting, very likely with tools and craftsmanship better than when the car was originally built in 1964. Note a piece of the original nose and headlight bucket sitting at the lower right.*

get the job done quickly and discreetly, insisting that the truck driver be prepared to drive it straight back with no other pick-ups, drop-offs, or stops.

He also went to his bank to gather the balance of the purchase price in cash, and in doing so, wiped out that branch's cash-on-hand. He nervously took a flight from San Francisco to Southern California to pay up and, he hoped, secure his prize. Then, he planned to rent a car to follow the transporter containing his rare Lamborghini all the way home and not let it out of his sight.

The only thing that would make this story creepier is if the car were stored in a dockside warehouse and the

transfer had to take place at 3:00 am in the fog with a Bogart-like character wearing a fedora and a trench coat.

Fortunately, the hand-off of money and paperwork as well as the load-up of the car went without a hitch or incident. The Lamborghini, now safe inside its truck, headed north toward San Francisco. A nervous Roesler followed close behind in his rental car, not wanting to stop or take his eyes off the truck for even a moment. He and his car arrived safely.

After a deeper investigation, Roesler began to realize fully what a special prize he'd won. The car came with a thick dossier of documentation, paperwork, letters, and other items testifying to the solidity of its importance and very early place in Lamborghini history, its early auto show appearances, and previous ownerships. With risk can come great reward.

Restoration Glory

Except for the front-end damage, this elegant silver bullet was complete and in generally good

The all-important data plate evidences the vehicle type as a 350 GT, and identifies this car, 0102, as the second production example built. This chassis, prior to the installation of the body, was displayed at the Geneva Motor Show in March 1964, proof that Lamborghini was serious about building a V-12–powered grand touring coupe.

Left: *The 350 GT's dash and instrument panel evolved over time, but this is the design in its purest form, with heavily chromed and polished instrumentation and neatly aligned rocker switches. Note the use of power window switches on the console; a rare and luxurious touch that many Ferraris and Maseratis did not yet have. But it was Signore Lamborghini's intent to show up his established, cross-town rivals.* **Right:** *The Jaeger instrumentation is beautifully detailed. The odometer was recently reset to zero miles, a practice not uncommon when a car is fully disassembled and completely restored. It's likely that the 300-kph top speed shown on this speedo is just a little optimistic, but maybe not by much.*

shape. Because it is such a rare and early car, Roesler knew that it deserved nothing less than a platinum-level, concours-quality full restoration. He entrusted that job to Symbolic Motor Cars of San Diego, California; Symbolic employee Bill Attaway led the charge on the job. The car was completely disassembled, and the team began repairing the front-end accident damage.

Roesler didn't intend to restore the car solely for high-level concours competition, but the 350 came out so beautifully that a tour of some of the world's most significant and prestigious car shows seemed the obvious path to take. The 0102 played hard and won big, competing at Monterey's ultra-prestigious Pebble Beach Concours d'Elegance, California's Concorso Italiano, and Italy's best known and superbly elegant Concorso d'Eleganza Villa d'Este held at the storied Villa d'Este Resort on the shores of Lake Como.

Roesler was more than honored by the invitation to display his rare car, once again looking factory fresh and original, in the rarefied air of these big-time concours. Fortunately, his expense, some extreme measures, and nerve-challenging efforts, as well as the efforts of Attaway and the Symbolic Motors team were rewarded with three first-in-class trophies. The once crashed, but now cherished, 350 GT won the Triple Crown of the world's great car shows.

Roesler has since sold the car to a noted car collector in Switzerland, not far from its birthplace in central Italy. Even though Roesler misses his very special Lamborghini, don't feel too sorry for him. He also has a rare Italian Iso Grifo in his garage that is also awaiting top-level restoration. But no overnight cash-only payments, foggy waterfronts, or trench-coated individuals were involved this time around.

Detailing like this wins you big hardware at major car shows. All of the stickers, decals, and production markings have been meticulously sourced or recreated by Attaway and the Symbolic crew, although it's highly likely that the restoration's standards of fit and finish exceed that of when the car was built new. Note the unique, wire-wrapped yellow fuel lines feeding the Weber carbs, which are mounted three per cylinder bank. The twin-choke carbs show that each cylinder has its own carburetor barrel.

Left: *Superleggera roughly translates to "super light," which is a method defined, if not exactly patented or invented, by Carrozzeria Touring in Milan. The idea behind it is a cage-like structure of thin steel tubing covered by aluminum body panels; it creates a relatively light, yet supremely strong body structure.* **Right:** *Lamborghini's original V-12 was designed primarily as a racing engine, although its power and spec were necessarily dialed back a bit for road-car duty. In this configuration, the dual overhead cam 3.5-liter V-12 is topped with six Weber carbs and rated for 280 hp at 6,500 rpm.*

The Bordeaux leather upholstery is set off by slightly brighter red carpeting, which perfectly replicates the original factory look. The 350 GT is nothing but a pure two-seater, while the original GTV prototype had one rear seat, and the later 400 GT was a 2+2. This car was designed to take a handsome, wealthy, jet-setting couple, and a minimum of luggage, off to someplace fabulous—in a hurry.

Perfectly recreated and carpeted panels define the cargo space; included is the proper period-looking tool roll. Factories often used "PROVA" license plates to indicate a vehicle's status as a prototype and allow it on the roads for development testing; these are from the Bologna, Italy, area. Even though the steeply raked rear window looks more like that of a hatchback, the trunk, as you can see, opens with a conventional closed metal deck lid.

Chapter 22

1965 Alfa Romeo Giulia 1600 Spider Veloce

ABSOLUTELY EXOTIC AND PURELY ITALIAN

All photos by Guido Bissattini ©2014, Courtesy of RM Auctions.

You may ask if this tidy Alfa Spider really qualifies as "exotic." Upon analysis, you'll see that, without question, it does. It's Italian to the core. It's from one of Italy's foremost marques with a great early history of fast, coachbuilt, high-performance cars. Not to mention Alfa Romeo's deep and considerable history in motorsport; don't forget that prior to forming his own legendary company, Enzo Ferrari managed Alfa's factory-supported Grand Prix team. The Spider wears designer coachwork, created and crafted by Pininfarina. And the engine is purely exotic; not so many cylinders, but with double overhead cam architecture, an aluminum head, and multiple side-draft carburation. Plus a sporty suspension and 5-speed manual transmission. Exotic stuff, for sure.

And the final icing on this particular little red roadster's cake is that it's the much rarer and higher performing Veloce model. The Veloce spec means it's a higher-performance version of Alfa's 1.6-liter (1,570 cc) straight-4 that is rated at 112 hp; the Normale version is only rated at 92 horses. This is all positively racy when you consider that the earlier Giulietta models ran 1,300-cc engines with 65 hp.

This dirt-covered brilliant-red example popped up at RM Auctions' Monaco sale in 2014. It wears chassis number AR 101 18 390417 and carries its original engine, number AR 00121 01950. It was among the final 600 ordered, and as its serial number indicates, it is a true Veloce (tipo 101 18).

The car was assembled on March 3, 1965, and then delivered new that summer to the Alfa Romeo dealer in Frankfurt, Germany. It was originally painted AR322 Sky Blue with a black interior, As you can see from these

A face that anyone could love; this Alfa was the design work of Pininfarina, the Turin design house and coachbuilder responsible for the look of countless great Alfas, Ferraris, Maseratis, and others.

photos, it's intact and complete, having lived its entire life in Europe.

RM had very little information on the car's life and history, other than the fact that it was obviously stored in a covered carport or woodshed for some years. Although it wasn't stored in an enclosed area, it has suffered little exposure to or damage from weather and the elements. The bodywork appears rot free, and the chrome is generally unblemished and free of rust.

It also appears that the car was stored with the hardtop in place, although the interior seems a bit worse for wear; the chrome gauge surrounds are rusty, and the surface of the instrument panel is peeling. There are no carpets, and the rest of the cabin is in slightly lumpy condition. The car was represented as a non-runner, but if it ran when parked, it is possible that a thorough

Twin overhead cams, hemi-head combustion chambers, and side-draft carbs with individual intake chokes replacing the factory air-cleaner housing; pretty exotic stuff, for sure.

Facing Page: *This is the dream of many Alfisti. A Veloce-spec Giulia Spider tucked neatly into a covered woodshed somewhere in Europe, dirty but complete and without rust, ready for sale and rescue from slumber.*

servicing and mechanical recommissioning (and some tidying work in the cabin) can bring it back to life without restoration or overhaul. It is likely that the rest of the car could be serviced and detailed, and this decidedly vintage bit of "La Dolce Vita" could be put back on the road with its history and patina intact.

That's what I'd do with it, although why not store that hardtop back in the barn, and cruise the byways of Italy and France al fresco? It's a Spider, designed for top-down fun on curvy mountain roads. String-back gloves, Persol sunglasses, and scarfs whipping in the wind.

This jewel-like Alfa was one of the least costly lots offered at RM's Monaco sale, and as such, drew much interest, spirited bidding, and a sale price of €44,800 (about $57,000). Although the car has needs, this must be considered a bit of a bargain, since prime examples routinely sell for much more than this.

Above: *Even though the car wasn't in an enclosed structure, it's likely that the space was relatively protected from the elements, for even though the car is covered with a fine layer of dirt, it doesn't appear to have ever gotten damp or waterlogged; the sure death of many a barn find, especially compact, open, steel-bodied roadsters such as this one.* **Below:** *The woodshed where the car lived faces a courtyard of sorts, surrounded by garages and other enclosed storage areas. Too bad this Alfa wasn't in one of them.*

Top Left: *The dash and instrumentation are all accounted for. The paint is peeling a bit and the chrome on the bezels around the gauges is pitted and rusty.* **Top Right:** *This Spider came from the factory with a black vinyl interior; this red piping was added at a later date and is not stock.* **Bottom Left:** *The original tag confirms the Veloce spec, body type, and serial number.* **Bottom Right:** *Another stamping on the chassis confirms the body's serial number.* **Below:** *The Giulia and its predecessor, the smaller engine Giulietta, boast a handsome and well-proportioned profile. Many of these cars were updated to run light alloy wheels, but certainly look just right wearing Alfa's vented steel wheels and trademark chromed hubcaps.*

Chapter 23

1965 Shelby GT350

EVEN AFTER NEARLY 50 YEARS, YOU *CAN* GO HOME AGAIN

The original Shelby Mustang GT350 of 1965 is among the foundations of the entire Shelby legacy. Of course the Cobra came first, but then Ford President Lee Iacocca asked Carroll Shelby to, in his words, "make a mule into a racehorse." Iacocca was as savvy an automotive executive as was ever born, and he knew that a youthful, sporty image helped sell cars. That is, of course, how the original Mustang came to be developed in the first place.

Shelby's idea was to take the Mustang's good basic underpinnings, spruce up the looks, amp up the performance, and then take it racing. The idea was to create a "Chevy beater" and an image car for Ford. The approach was straightforward and very effective. Take a lightweight, modestly equipped Mustang GT 2+2 "fastback" and juice up the horsepower by about 34 ponies, remove the back seat to turn the Mustang into a two-seater "sport" car (as Shelby called them), improve the handling, sex it up a little, and call it the Shelby GT350.

Automatic transmission? Nope. Air conditioning? Not a chance. Corvette-beating performance? Absolutely.

Shelby American built just 562 of these rough-and-ready 1965 models, and each successive year, the original GT350's mix of race-bred performance was toned down just a smidge. The automatic transmission and optional air conditioning came along soon enough, along with much larger engines. By 1967 the car got larger and heavier. In addition, pending air pollution regulations began to diminish performance as the 1960s wound down. Now that's not to say that any 1965–1970 Shelby Mustang isn't a rare, sought after, and now expensive collector car, but the dyed-in-the-wool Shelby purists put the original 1965 right at the front of the herd.

Burt Boeckmann's Southern California–based Galpin Ford sold a lot of Mustangs in the mid-1960s. A lot. And when a Shelby guy came along offering a hopped-up Mustang as a way to sell more of them, Boeckmann became one of the first Shelby Mustang dealers in America. And Galpin sold a lot of *Shelby* Mustangs too, including 1965 GT350 chassis 5S492.

Roundabout Journey Back Home

This car was the quintessential 1965 Shelby: Wimbledon White with metallic Blue Shelby stripes up and over the hood, roof, and deck. Optional Shelby Cragar mag wheels, loud side-exit exhaust pipes, 305-hp "Hi-Po" 289 with all the Shelby hop-up goodies in place, including the rare optional finned aluminum oil pan.

Galpin had the car, 5S492, in stock from Shelby American. Then in a dealer-trade sale transaction, the car went to Webster Ford in Caruthers, California, which

This angle shows the proper 1965 GT350 hood scoop as it should be. All of the exterior paint and panels are original on this amazing time-warp Shelby.

then sold it to its first retail owner on September 29, 1965. Even though Galpin didn't sell this car new as a retail unit, 5S492 absolutely passed through its dealership turnstiles on its way to its first owner. Sometime in the early 1970s, it was parked in a suburban California garage and the engine was removed for freshening, with the odometer sitting somewhere around 44,000 miles.

And it sat. And sat. Then sat some more.

With the passage of time, it became clear to the owners that the car wasn't likely to be restored or put back on the road any time soon. Selling it seemed like a good idea. Consigning it to Arizona's Barrett-Jackson Auction Company as one of the stars of its 2012 Scottsdale Arizona collector car auction sale turned out to be another brilliant idea.

This was about the time that the whole barn-find phenomenon began to really gain traction. Barrett-Jackson chairman Craig Jackson and company president Steve Davis are serious muscle car experts, and both are longtime friends of Carroll Shelby. They knew that this rough-looking gem represented a marketing opportunity of Hope Diamond proportions. The car, matching-numbers powertrain, and miscellaneous parts were rescued from the garage. The car was reassembled and serviced to put it in complete and running condition; they were careful not to remove any important and still serviceable original parts.

The car was offered for auction sale at no reserve, clearly one of the stars of Barrett-Jackson's 2012 sale. The Shelby community buzzed: Who would buy this car? What would be the selling price? And would the new owner restore it or leave it in its somewhat timeworn but spectacularly original condition?

The answers are Beau Boeckmann, the son of Galpin's Bert Boeckmann, who is now president of the Galpin Auto Collection and is now in charge of the Galpin dealership dynasty. He paid $385,000, and no, the car will not be taken apart and restored to any sort of concours condition.

I was present when the car was auctioned on that January Saturday in Arizona, and nearly all of the oxygen escaped Barrett-Jackson's massive tent when the bidding passed $200,000. Beau Boeckmann wasn't present (he was in an airplane on a business trip), but one of his first lieutenants, Dave Shuten, a longtime friend and trusted employee, was there to bid on Galpin's behalf.

After the sale concluded and it was clear that Galpin had won the car, I congratulated Shuten on bringing the car "home to Galpin." Referring to the likely record price for a somewhat rundown 1965 Mustang, he replied, "I'm either a hero, or I'm going to be fired."

Facing Page: *The profile, colors, and stripe graphics of an early GT350 are immediately recognizable. This car sits right on all four corners, looking ready for any road or track on proper-size Goodyear Blue Dot Special tires wrapped around rare and desirable Shelby/Cragar two-piece mags. It's a car for all times and all reasons, and a muscle car look that's never wrong. Exotic? Absolutely.*

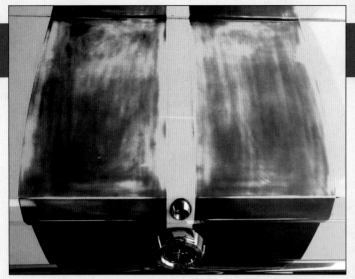

Left: *The original Guardsman Blue Shelby Stripes, the brilliant vision by Shelby American's chief designer Peter Brock, is a seminal look that changed little on Shelby Mustangs throughout the years. It's still available on new Shelby Mustangs. As you can tell from this photo, they were painted on top of the factory Wimbledon White paint job. On this car they have been worn and polished nearly all the way through to the underlying paint. Repaint them to new and perfect? I say no way; why scrub off this historic car's stories? The Boeckmann family agrees.* **Top Right:** *This timeworn original badge is on the passenger's side of the rear-deck fascia, right where it belongs.* **Bottom Right:** *The all-important Shelby underhood identification and VIN plate; its faded appearance and worn rivets indicate that the plate has never been removed or otherwise messed with. This is hugely important when it comes to verifying a vehicle's provenance and maximizing its value to discerning collectors.*

To Restore or Not To Restore

The car is an amazing physical specimen: original white paint and blue stripes, a mildly worn interior, but overall complete, and in great shape. All the rare steel/aluminum wheels are in place (amazingly including the spare) as well as very expensive and difficult-to-replace items such as the wood-rimmed, aluminum-spoked steering wheel and the Cobra head–shaped tach and gauge cluster mounted on the dash just above the radio.

The exterior paint has a few bangs and scrapes from its early days on the dragstrip, and the blue stripes have been waxed and polished through to the underlying primer, white paint, and even metal in a few places. The car wears lots of event stickers and badges testifying to its attendance at a wide variety of mid- to late-1960s club

The car's uncluttered original interior is mildly faded but still looks ready for business. Note the lack of a console, the add-on air-conditioning unit, and the presence of competition-style lap belts. There's little doubt that this car took a few road course laps at full throttle as well as some passes down the quarter-mile just for good measure.

Left: *Original and slightly beat up, the rear license plate and metal Galpin license plate frame are important elements of the car's presentation, along with great wheels and period-looking tires. It looks as if, during its first life, the car was last registered in 1974, likely about when it came down for engine work, and a long, long sleep until it was reunited with Galpin Ford in 2012.* **Middle:** *Remember that the GT350 was homologated as a two-seat sports car, so there is no back seat. Instead, the resulting package shelf makes a handy place to keep the spare, in this case not just a black-stamped steel wheel, but another of those great-looking Cragar Shelby mags, in this case visible through the rear window. The only thing that would make this cooler would be a leather belt–strap holding down a four-pointed-star lug wrench, a look common in racing and rally cars of the 1960s.* **Right:** *More evidence of some days spent living life one quarter-mile at a time are stickers from Southern California's famous, now defunct, Lions Drag Strip as well as the American Hot Rod Association drag racing sanctioning body. Even though the GT350 was primarily intended for SCCA B Production road racing duty, they were great drag racers, being relatively lightweight Mustangs with manual transmissions and high-revving, solid-lifter V-8 engines.*

and racing events. Its original period-correct California black and gold license plates are intact.

When these photos were taken, the speedo read 44,945 original miles. The engine fires easily with a sharp, barking report from its glasspack mufflers and side-exhaust dumps that exit just in front of the rear wheels. The clutch and the manual steering are a little heavy, and the car is absolutely honest in every way.

I asked Beau Boeckmann if he ever planned to restore the car to pristine, unmarked beauty. His reply was an enthusiastic, "No way! It's beautiful exactly the way it is!" Therefore, it becomes an originality template or pattern car for any owner or restorer wishing to restore a 1965 Shelby to absolute, NOS, as-delivered original condition.

After buying the car, Boeckmann said his goal was to drive it from his Southern California home to Monterey

The Galpin GT350 takes pride of place at the Galpin Auto Collection museum with a beaming Beau Boeckmann (right) and Galpin Auto Sport's general manager Steve McCord (left). The Galpin collection houses many fine, original Shelby Mustangs and Cobras, several of which were originally sold new by the company.

Left: *This rare and costly wood-and-aluminum steering wheel is now being reproduced, but this one is no repop piece; it shows just enough gentle wear and tarnish to evidence it as the car's original wheel. The 1965 instrument panel still has the early band-style Mustang speedo. Talk about a handsome, unadorned, and businesslike office made strictly for the business of going fast.* **Right:** *Some experts opine that this housing for the Shelby tach and oil pressure gauge was designed to resemble the head of a rearing Cobra snake. Whether or not this is true, it's a cool piece, and a must on any 1965 GT350. Originals such as this one are worth many thousands of dollars. Note the simple AM radio and Mustang club event dash plaques just below it.*

Left: *This sticker is humorous but the real gold here is the odometer, reading just 44,945.1 miles to date from new. The car's condition is consistent with this mileage, especially given its long rest in a garage with no engine onboard.* **Middle:** *Even though the paint is original, it doesn't mean it hasn't been spot touched up here and there. This lower rear valance shows some scrapes, scratches, as well as some home-style brush and spray paint touch-up attempts. You could certainly make this car more pristine, but it could never be made more original.* **Right:** *Along the way, someone attempted to paint Cobra lettering onto the hoodscoop. It wasn't done very well, and hasn't lasted the test of time, but it is nonetheless part of the car's story and history.*

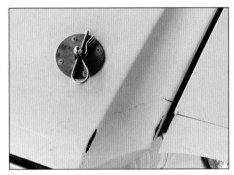

Left: *The original hood paint shows its share of nicks and scrapes, but the car's panel fit and shut lines are generally straight, or at least to 1965 standards. Hood pins are OEM Shelby pieces.* **Middle:** *I can't tell for sure if this Rotunda oil filter is an NOS piece or a reproduction, but this is what they looked like in 1965, long before the Motorcraft or Ford Racing pieces. Nice period touch.* **Right:** *As you'd expect, the stripes on the horizontal surfaces show the most wear. These side stripes mounted low on the rocker panels have stood the test of time, polishing, and sun with comparatively little wear or fading.*

GT 350 OFFERS FINEST IN STYLING, PERFORMANCE, PRACTICALITY

IT LOOKS FAST FROM EVERY ANGLE—This is the Mustang GT 350, which combines the finest in sports car performance with stock car practicality. It is on display at Galpin Ford, which has a greater number of Mustang models than any other Southern California Ford dealer.

Galpin Ford Awarded Franchise for GT 350

"The Americanization of Carroll Shelby" or "How I Made Horace Wink Blink" has opened for an indefinite run at Galpin Ford.

These are apt titles for the debut of the Mustang GT 350,

Galpin Offers Advantages

the phenomenal fastback which internationally famed race car builder Carroll Shelby is converting for high performance sports car competition.

Galpin Ford, which for the last four years has sponsored cars in West Coast NASCAR competition and won the season high-point championship each of those years, is the first Southern California Ford dealer to be awarded a Mustang GT 350 franchise. Galpin also will handle Shelby's Ford Cobra sports

car.

Galpin Ford's spectacular success in stock car racing competition is emblematic of the high standard of mechanical knowhow of the Galpin Ford Service Dept., and makes Galpin Ford the logical choice to inaugurate the merchandising of the Mustang GT 350.

The GT 350 offers racing car suspension, disc brakes, 15-inch wheels, performance-tuned 289 Cobra engine, limited-slip rear end and race-bred interior.

for the annual Monterey Car Week held each August; the events include the Pebble Beach Concours d'Elegance, the Rolex Monterey Motorsports Reunion, a variety of OEM and dealer activities that he must attend, as well as several other shows, and club and race gatherings.

Upon taking delivery of the car after the January 2012 auction, his Galpin Auto Sports crew continued massaging and fettling the car, not with any intent to cosmetically improve, alter, or restore it, but only to ensure that it was in top mechanical condition for the trip he had planned later that summer of 1,000 or so miles. And he did it, driving the car from the San Fernando Valley to Monterey, around to various events, and then home, with no meaningful problems or breakdowns.

Beau's father Bert, the patriarch of the Boeckmann family and of Galpin Ford, has an interesting take on this car: "I usually agree with my son on most of the decisions we make around the business, but this one I just don't understand. I told him 'Son, why would you spend so much money on this Mustang that's all dirty and beat up? We used to sell them brand new for about $5,000, in perfect condition.'"

Bert has, however, since come around to agree that the car is something special to Galpin's history. Times change; some people embrace the barn-find experience, and some just don't.

Top: *The 1965 GT350 engine bay looks only a little less shiny, but probably very much as it did the day it rolled out of Shelby's Los Angeles-area production factory. You can see the Shelby identification plate riveted to the top driver-side inner fender well, near where the Ford factory VIN is stamped. Just as it should be. Notice Shelby American's use of two different pieces meant to improve chassis structural rigidity. One was the triangulation brace, originally developed for convertible Mustangs, which ties the shock towers to the firewall. The other was the all-important "Monte Carlo bar" that further supports the shock towers while flexing in or out during high-load cornering.* **Middle:** *"All this, for around $5,000." Galpin was among the first Shelby American dealers. The Boeckmann family and Carroll Shelby were long-time close friends as well as successful business associates.* **Bottom:** *Back home again, in Gardena, California, not Indiana. The Galpin GT350 visits what is now called Shelby Los Angeles, where Carroll had an office, most of his own personal car collection, and his Goodyear Racing Tire distributorship. The low-lying industrial property now holds parent company Carroll Shelby International, Shelby Licensing, and the Carroll Shelby Foundation. Plans are afoot to remodel the property into a museum celebrating the life and cars of the late, great, Carroll.*

Chapter 24

1966 Jaguar 4.2-Liter Series 1 E-Type Coupe

CHANGING THE E-TYPE, BUT CAN YOU MAKE IT BETTER?

All photos courtesy of Evan Klein.

This startling XKE coupe is one of two Jaguars restyled and customized by world-renowned industrial and automotive designer Raymond Loewy (it is the only one remaining; the other was created from a 1955 XK140, which was demolished in a fire in 1957). Pichon-Parat of Sens, France, accomplished the substantial coachwork redesign on this E-Type. The car was owned and driven by Loewy while he lived in France and Monaco.

Loewy's accomplishments are many and varied; he designed everything from office equipment to locomotives. His portfolio includes the uniquely tapered Coke bottle, and among his well-known current and past logo designs are those of British Petroleum (BP), the Shell Oil Company, and the United States Postal Service. His best known automotive design work was for Studebaker, including his assembly and spearheading of the team that designed the Studebaker Avanti of the early 1960s.

The E-Type, or XKE, has a history that is the stuff of automotive legend. This fabulous sports car was sold from 1961 through 1974 in three body styles and was powered by either the race-proven twin-cam XK straight-6-cylinder engine or, later, by a 5.3-liter single overhead cam V-12. Collectors tend to favor the early 6-cylinder models in coupe or roadster form. The E-Type that Loewy purchased and chose to redesign falls into that category, being a "second generation" Series I coupe with the 4.2-liter engine and a manual transmission.

The E-Type was styled by Jaguar owner and patron Sir William Lyons and aerodynamicist/designer Malcolm Sayer (although Sayer always insisted his cars were designed by the wind, not really by his hand or idea). Of course, the car has long been considered a design icon, with examples on display in countless museums and collections around the world; many consider it to be among the most beautiful sports car designs ever. Who could argue?

Loewy deserves a certain amount of credit for having the guts and gumption to attempt to improve upon the E-Type's sinuous, feline shape and detailing. Did he improve it or not? It's a matter of personal taste. His redesign contains many interesting details, and it certainly changes the looks of the car, even though you'd never mistake it for something other than an E-Type.

Loewy's E-Type was left mechanically stock; his redesign work was restricted to the body panels, side window openings, and glass. The car was shortened fore (25 cm) and aft (12 cm), and the new nose encompassed a dual headlight treatment; the quad lights were mounted behind plastic covers, which was the current fashion in the

The E-Type's standard metal-and-glass rear hatch opens to reveal an otherwise stock interior, except for his rendition of a high-mounted stoplight on the driver's side. The addition of a large, chrome, plug-in flashlight on the dashboard near the shifter is visible here. The stock interior is dirty and mildly worn, but is complete and otherwise in good condition.

mid-1960s. The car's original radiator opening was also dispensed with in favor of a large oval-shaped metal grille, which likely improved the E-Type's marginal cooling capacity.

The factory taillights were replaced with Chevrolet Corvair units frenched into the quarter panels, and the dual exhaust pipes that normally exit just below the rear license plate splay outward exiting the tail of the car at approximately 45 degree angles. A unique glass "spoiler" was mounted at the trailing edge of the roof.

Loewy anticipated today's Center High-Mounted Stoplight regulations by placing a large, red taillight in the aft cabin; it was activated by the brake pedal and was visible through the 25-percent-larger (than stock) rear window. The interior remains otherwise stock. At the time these photos were taken, in 2010, the car was original and exactly as designed by Loewy and constructed by Pichon-Parat. I drove it briefly, and it felt in generally solid mechanical condition, although it needed servicing and brake system refurbishment.

The car was consigned for auction sale by the family of the third owner, the late architect and automotive designer James Murray Hunt, who studied under Loewy early in his career. At some point, Loewy sold the car to another individual in France, who owned it for some time, before advertising it in *The New York Times* (or *The Wall Street Journal*). Hunt spotted the advertisement in 1970, purchased the car sight unseen, and imported it to San Diego, California, where he owned it for the rest of his life.

It spent 40 years hidden away in Hunt's garage and was considered lost to much of the motoring community. The custom one-off, designed by Raymond Loewy, was offered publicly for sale for the first time since 1970, at a Bonhams auction in mid-2011. It sold for $128,000 including buyer's premiums and commissions.

I've learned that the new owner did not enjoy the car's patina and originality, and has since given it new paint and a full cosmetic restoration, which makes me think that Loewy would either be proud or disappointed.

Loewy's redesign touched nearly every angle of the car, in this case swapping the stock taillights with smaller, round Corvair pieces. The stock exhaust system was retained, but the rear mufflers were remounted to exit the rear of the car just below the taillights, instead of their stock locations just below the rear license plate.

Facing Page: *Even though this feline shape could be none other than an E-Type, Raymond Loewy's redesign certainly changed its look; some like it, some don't. The dual headlights were in fashion at the time, the large grille is distinctive, and the front hood scoop and reconfigured rear window treatment make it look like a very different automobile.*

Chapter 25

1967 Lamborghini Miura

THE ULTIMATE EXOTIC SUFFERS THE ULTIMATE NEGLECT

All photos courtesy of Wayne Carini and Crashing Wave Entertainment.

*A*uthor's note: Wayne Carini is one of the world's great car guys. An accomplished restoration shop owner, specialty car dealer, concours judge, and collector car consultant, Carini is the host of Discovery/ Velocity Network's popular *Chasing Classic Cars* reality television series. During the opening of each episode, Carini declares, "I chase cars. I buy them. And I sell them. And it's all about the chase."

In fact Carini does much more than that, but the nature of his business and this show make him among the ultimate barn finders, and his pursuits lead him all around the world in search of the next great find. Sometimes, Carini buys the car(s) himself either to keep in his personal collection, or to restore and resell. Other times,

he advises a family about how best to sell or otherwise manage cars that have been left behind by the passing of older family members. He often represents buyers in their seeking and purchase of a great car.

Regardless of the circumstances, Carini's business and life always put him in touch with great cars and their stories. More directly here, Wayne Carini is my friend, and is gracious enough to share this amazing Lamborghini supercar garage-find story with me for this book. You can learn more about Carini, his dealership, and restoration shop, as well as his highly engaging television show at f40.com.

The Lamborghini Miura came along at an interesting time in the history of modern exotic cars. The mid-1960s was an era of discovery, innovation, and exploration; it wasn't yet clear which path was best for a modern high-performance sports car: the traditional front-engine, rear-wheel-drive configuration or a pure mid-engine layout, with the engine mounted just aft of the driver and passenger compartment, yet contained within the wheelbase of the car. This is in contrast to a technically rear-engine layout, where much of or the entire engine sits behind the rear axle line, such as with a Porsche 911 or a Corvair. The prevailing logic at the time, certainly by Enzo Ferrari, at least, maintained that a classic front-engine, rear-drive layout was better for a road-going machine, while the notion of a mid-engine machine was best for the racetrack.

Ferruccio Lamborghini felt different, and was eager to develop a road-going mid-engine exotic to augment his growing line of high-end gran turismos. The company's

Above: *Imagining tugging open a pair of stubborn barn doors and finding this. It's the real deal: An early Euro-spec Lamborghini Miura, stacked on blocks, complete but filthy. The original exotic supercar; this goes on any list of the world's greatest barn finds.*

Facing Page: *Looking down this rural alleyway, you'd never guess at the magic behind the doors. With them wrestled open, you can just see the tail of the car sticking out. Carini wasn't the first to discover this hidden "Hope Diamond," but hopes to be the lucky one to take it home and nurse it back to running perfection.*

first mid-engine V-12–powered chassis was displayed at the 1965 Turin Auto Show, with no bodywork covering the underpinnings. Many showgoers and media members assumed it was the underpinnings of a racing car, perhaps along the lines of the Ford GT40. Absolutely not the case. The questions were answered for good just a few months later when Lamborghini rolled out the Marcello Gandini–designed Miura concept at the 1966 Geneva Motor Show.

The Miura was startling; its low, sensuous, and perfectly proportioned bodywork, with the V-12 mounted transversely just aft of the passenger compartment, was tied to a 5-speed manual transaxle. The car was in production for the 1966 model year; its V-12 engine was a slightly reconfigured version of the company's then-current 3.5-liter V-12. In the Miura, it was rated at 350 hp. Performance was impressive even from the beginning, although the car suffered a variety of engineering teething problems.

Gian Paolo Dallera, Paolo Stanzini, and development testing driver Bob Wallace, were all responsible for the car's initial development. They kept working on the design, smoothing out its flaws, and making it an ever more impressive performer as time went along. There were multiple evolutions throughout the car's production life, and it is reputed that England's *CAR* magazine was speaking specifically of the Miura when it coined the term "supercar." Just 764 of the various Miura models were produced from 1966 to 1973, and today it is among the world's most valuable and sought-after Italian exotic cars.

A Garage-Find Countach Wannabe Kit Car? Nope

Wayne Carini was recently introduced to a spectacular barn-fresh 1967 Miura, in the proverbial single-car garage, and here is how he tells the story:

"I must get 20 messages a day about cars that are for sale or that someone has found and think that I might be interested in. They range all over the board from brass-era cars to American cars of the 1940s and 1950s to exotics. They are in people's garages, barns, and sometimes even their basements. They are all intriguing, but some much more so than others.

"I usually have lunch in my office and go through the morning messages and emails, hoping to find the special message containing that hidden treasure. As I'm going through my messages on this particular day I read, 'Lamborghini on cement blocks, garage door falling off, call for more information.'

"This type of message often ends up being a wild goose chase through someone's back yard, with the 'Lamborghini' being a poorly assembled Countach-wannabe kit car. I plow through the rest of the messages, and nothing seems particularly hot or needs immediate attention so after lunch I'm back to work painting a car in the shop. I

This brilliant orange is the car's factory color and paint job; in spite of all the dust and spiderwebs, it appears to have survived well. Carini will certainly detail and preserve all of the car's original finishes if he acquires the car. Bright primary-style non-metallic paint colors were a Lamborghini trademark in the 1960s, and remain so today.

get about halfway through spraying the first coat of clear, and all the while I'm thinking about the mysterious Lamborghini message.

"Could it be true?

"I finish the first coat and run to the phone. I make the call . . . and get an answering machine. After leaving the message, I head back to work, and in my mind, I'm beginning to picture an abandoned Lamborghini sitting up on blocks. I'm still in the booth applying more paint, when my assistant holds up a little sign in the spray booth window for me: 'Lambo guy's on the phone.' Sorry, but the paint's gotta wait.

"As I ran for the phone. I tried to curb my excitement and collect my emotions, because after all, it's probably just another false lead on a great car or a real lead on a dumb one. I take the call and it's a guy who works as a letter carrier, and claims he knows of a Lamborghini Miura (!) in a garage down an alleyway and that the older gent who owns it is thinking about selling it.

"I ask him to send me some photos by email and he replies that the owner doesn't want it exposed on the Internet and so hasn't allowed any photos, but that if I am interested, I can come down and take a look. Interested?

"Are you kidding?! I ask him how soon I can visit and we set a time for the next day. I also ask if I can bring the *Chasing Classic Cars* camera crew to document the find, although he was concerned that doing so might spook the guy. No matter, I said I'd see him the next afternoon.

"I was on the phone, right away, to my production team and explained all about the car, adding that there was some concern that if we show up with cameras and lights blazing it might spook the owner a little, and that we may, or may not, be able to film the event. I didn't want to disrespect this very private and now somewhat elderly gentleman, but that issue wasn't going to stop me from going there with the intent of buying the car.

"We decided to bring the crew and see if we could gently talk the owner into letting us film the find. The chase was on, and the next morning, my crew and I were on an airplane in search of Lamborghini reality, or disappointment. We didn't know which.

Facing Page Top: *Of course it's only logical that this quaint property would be wrapped by a white picket fence, with flowers all around it. Fortunately, the car was stacked on blocks on a cement, rather than dirt, floor that protected it from the area's harsh winters. It is equally good luck that all of the rare, knock-off Campagnolo wheels are safely in the garage.* **Facing Page Bottom:** *Imagine having this screaming orange zonker as your everyday ride to and from work; for many years that was owner Jay's reality. The original air cleaners were found floating around in the garage rubbish. Carini was pleased to see how complete and original the car is.*

Left: *A face like no other and Gandini's masterpiece for sure. Note the metal "eyelashes" surrounding the flip-up head-lights; it's a charming if only slightly hokey design cue, which was deleted later in the Miura's production life.* **Right:** *These engine cover slats are factory correct in every way; they allow some heat to escape the tightly packed engine compartment yet keep out dirt and rain. It's a great look that's been replicated on many other cars, most notably the 1970 Ford Mustang Boss 302.*

"We met our intermediary, the postal worker, a few miles away from the property. Based on his description, it sounded accurate and pretty real on the surface. His plan was to lead us to the owner's quaint property about 2 miles away. By now, my excitement level was redlining, and I found myself running through several very late yellow lights trying to make sure I didn't lose our guide.

"We pulled down an alley, next to an average-looking house and garage, and of course my heart was pounding. This was the place, claimed our friend. So I asked our camera team to leave the equipment in the rental car for now and not to mention anything about television or filming.

"An older gent comes out of the house, and we're introduced. I'll call him Jay, and he immediately asked if I'm ready to see the car. Well, duh! My semi-calm reply was 'yes, please.' He added that the doors were a bit tricky to open and that it would take him just a minute. I offered to help but he said there was a method to it and no help was needed.

"I sensed that this was an appropriate moment to ask him about filming, because we wanted to get the opening of the doors and unveiling of the car on film. Not sure what to say, I just popped the question: 'Jay, would you mind if I filmed this for a television show I do?'

"After a very pregnant pause he replied, "Sure, I guess that would be okay."

"Cameraman Jim blazed back to the car to get his gear, while I tried to slow down the garage door opening process until the cameras were ready and rolling. It felt as if we were cracking the door to King Tut's tomb; I had goose bumps all over.

"As the final section of the door creaked open, I saw it. The real thing. A fabulously bright and equally dusty orange 1967 Miura, wheels removed, sitting on cinderblocks. No fake Countach here. An early-spec and very original looking Lamborghini Miura. Be still my beating heart.

"I nervously asked the owner if we could go in and get a closer look. Considering this group of people, cameras, and bright lights invading his private space, he was most accommodating. I was, of course, looking primarily at the car, yet already trying to figure out how I could get it moved and transported, because I had no desire to leave until we'd made a deal for me to buy it.

"As we gingerly walked around the car, the owner began to tell me that he had parked it in this garage a few years ago to repair the brakes, which were binding and hanging up, and that he had taken the wheels off but that's as far as he'd been able to go. My inspection proved that the car was very intact except for the air cleaners that Jay had modified. I was already sure that this was one of my greatest ever finds, and I asked him to tell me a bit more about the car's history, which only got better.

"Jay said that the car was previously owned by Ford Motor Company, and that he had purchased the car via a newspaper ad. He continued that Ford had purchased the car new and had it shipped from Italy so its engineers could study the car. After the engineers were finished with it, they put an ad in a local paper where Jay's brother read it. Jay told me that he was an electrical engineer and used to drive this car to work every day during the summer months. He said that he has had several people wanting to buy the car. I got a little flushed about that time, as I realized that I'm not the first to find this treasure.

"There never seems to be a good time to talk money, so why not now? So I asked, 'Jay, how much are you asking for the car?'

"And then I got the dreaded answer: 'Oh, it's not for sale.'

After watching the garage door opening procedure in reverse, and seeing the car disappear back into hiding, I became ever more determined to try to talk Jay into selling me the rare Lamborghini. We walked to the front of the house, and I asked if he'd ever seen my television show, *Chasing Classic Cars*? He said that he had not because he didn't watch much television. I told him that it was on cable, and he said he didn't have cable! Then I noticed a satellite dish on his roof. But, of course, it was nonfunctional. I told him I'd send him DVDs of the show so he could watch it, but he said he didn't have a DVD player. Oy! So of course I offered to send him not only the DVDs, but also a DVD player, so he could watch it.

"As we spoke, I tried my very best to convince him to sell me the car, and then realized something important. It then struck me that this car represented a huge piece of Jay's life. It's something that people wanted to see and talk about with him. It brought him back to a younger age and time when the car was running and was, in fact, his everyday driver for much of the year. This car was one of his connections to the world, and without it he would lose that.

"I left his house that day without the car but with a good feeling that when the time is right, I have a good chance to go back to that garage and relive the moment of finding the car all over again, and finally exhuming it from a long dusty slumber.

"Jay and I stay in touch. He finally got cable and has become a fan of *Chasing Classic Cars*. I look forward to his phone call telling me it's time to come and take the Lamborghini out of the garage and back home with me. Until that time, I will be paying closer attention to my emails and phone messages, ready for the next great chase to begin."

"But not today." On his first visit, Carini rightly judged that the seller just wasn't ready to let the car go yet. But given the gentle assurance that he would be the right caretaker for the car, it's quite likely that the owner will come back to Wayne when the time is right.

Chapter 26

1967 Ferrari 330 GTS

A FERRARI SO GOOD THAT EVEN FIRE COULDN'T REALLY HURT IT

The late Dean Batchelor, a seriously credentialed automotive designer, racer, journalist, and author with three notable Ferrari books to his credit, once told me that the 275/330/365 GTC/GTS series of Ferraris were the best driving, most user friendly, and most reliable among all Ferrari V-12 models ever made. And he was one to know, absolutely qualified to make that assessment as a Ferrari owner and expert, and as a previous editor-in-chief of *Road & Track* magazine.

The 330 GTC (gran turismo coupe) and 330 GTS (gran turismo spyder, or convertible) were new for 1966, and shared considerable chassis architecture and mechanicals with the highly successful and desirable 275 GTB (gran turismo berlinetta, or coupe). The 330 boasted a slightly larger engine than the 275. It was still a single overhead cam V-12 topped by Weber carbs, but in this case, it was a 4.0-liter unit rated at 300 hp.

The new coupe and convertible were designed by Pininfarina, and could be thought of as only slightly less racy than the 275 GTB, but formidable performers nonetheless. The cabins are luxuriously trimmed in leather and wood, the car really targeted at high-speed grand touring. The body shape is a little more conservative than the 275 GTB's somewhat GTO-like profile, and the suspension is tuned for a slightly better ride quality.

Like most Ferraris (then and now), it was an expensive car at around $15,000. Both the coupe and the spyder are very attractive; the spyder is particularly elegant with the top down. Ferrari built just 99 330 series GTS convertibles; this example, chassis 9343 GT, is the fifth one produced in the model run.

Its color combination, Celeste Blue over dark red leather interior, is particularly rare and elegant. The car was imported to and sold by Luigi Chinetti's factory Ferrari dealership in Connecticut. Dr. Samuel Scher of New York City purchased it new in April 1967. Scher was a considerable car enthusiast, and throughout his life, assembled an impressive collection of premium automobiles. He drove this exquisite Ferrari approximately 20,000 miles in the first two years he owned it.

In the summer of 1969, the car suffered an engine bay fire (relatively small as engine fires go), which did some underhood damage and blistered the paint on the trailing edge of the hood and front fender on the driver's side. The damage was enough to take the car off the road, and for some reason, the Ferrari was considered a total loss. The insurance company subsequently sold it at auction on September 16, 1969.

You'd have to look hard to find a more balanced, well-proportioned open-topped Ferrari sports car design than the 275/330/365 GTC/GTS. It represented the best of Pininfarina's mid-1960s portfolio and looks great in almost any color combination.

The next owner apparently intended to restore the car. However, for reasons not discovered, the project stalled, and was never completed. The owner's detailed typewritten list of parts needed to do the job, along with the car's books, manuals, and other records remained in the trunk. Most amazing.

Thus, this nearly new and now rare Ferrari spyder sat untouched in a Pennsylvania garage for 44 years until Gooding & Company consigned it for sale at its Scottsdale, Arizona, classic car auction in January 2014.

Seeing it in the metal is inspiring and sad at the same time. Inspiring because it's in almost time-warp condition, having suffered no rust or accident damage, and, as seen in these photos, the odometer registered a mere 36,717 kilometers, or just 22,815 miles. Sad because of all the great miles its previous owners didn't get to enjoy driving it and, of course, because of its damaged and rather tatty looking condition. But the real beauty lies beneath. The 9343 is absolutely original in every way, with its engine

Somewhere beneath all this crud is a gleaming jewel of a Ferrari spyder. Original five-decade-old Celeste Blue paint remains but could certainly stand a high-quality color sand and buff job. All of the original chrome and badging is in place and in generally good condition.

Facing Page: *Given the shapes of the rear fenders and the slightly recessed trunk line, some have likened this three-quarter rear view to that of a slightly larger scale Fiat 124 Spyder, which is also a Pininfarina design. However, the two cars are only very remotely connected. The 124 was primarily the work of American-born designer Tom Tjaarda; although he was at Pininfarina, his direct fingerprints are not found on the Ferrari GTS.*

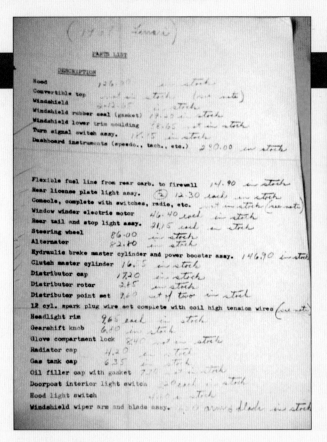

Left: *Another valuable piece found in the trunk is this annotated list of replacement parts needed to put the car back on the road after the fire damage. It's doubtful that these parts could be bought new today for anywhere close to the prices on this shopping list from the late 1960s or early 1970s.* **Right:** *The interior is mostly complete and in generally good shape, although the moths ate the carpeting long ago and, for some reason, the air vents in the center console have been removed. The genuine wood rim is clean and not cracked or faded, and the leather seats can likely be deep oil treated and brought back to life. And obviously, a new windshield is in order here.*

and all other numbers matching. It's never suffered from a ham-fisted restoration, color change, or been spoiled or soiled in any other way.

I asked David Gooding if this is a car that should be mechanically recommissioned, detailed, serviced, and put back on the road as a "preservation" example or if it would only ever again be proper and truly beautiful after a complete, concours-level restoration. The thoughtful and well-spoken Gooding replied, "That's a tough one. Because, of course, being so complete and original, it would be a perfect starting palette for a platinum-level restoration. Yet, if you start picking away at the paint or

chrome with a rag and a little water, the factory finishes are in really good shape underneath all the dirt.

"You'd want to repaint the hood and fender where the fire blistered the paint, but other than that, I believe this car would detail up beautifully. So the next owner will have a choice and won't be wrong, ending up with a fabulous car, either way." The next owner will certainly have a thrilling machine, regardless of the approach chosen.

In its August 1968 330 GTS road test, *Road & Track* said: "Ferrari continues to progress toward the perfect sports car. The 330 GTS is not just a wonderful, exciting open roadster, but also a comfortable . . . everyday car that doesn't mind being driven to the supermarket. If it's still tough to justify that $15,000 tag, just remember that you can't get anything like it for any less."

That $15,000 investment, in 1968, would have been a rather prudent buy, given that this amazing barn-find original 330 GTS sold in January 2014 (in damaged, non-running condition) for $2,062,000.

All of the Ferrari's Borrani RW4039 knock-off wire wheels are present and undamaged; they just need a serious cleaning, truing, and balancing. This model could also be had with knock-off alloys, but the wires just look so right on this elegant convertible. Dr. Scher displayed considerable taste when he ordered this car.

Top Left: *The fire damage is just visible at the upper left corner; it singed some wiring and patches of paint on the hood and driver-side fender. Note Ferrari V-12's symmetrical-looking dual distributors (six cylinders per bank) and dual oil filters; only the driver's side is functional.* **Top Right:** *Now that's great junk in the trunk; the previous owners were careful enough to keep the car's books, manuals, papers, and records with the car. They are a real bonus to its appeal, provenance, and value.* **Below:** *The dusty Ferrari looks a bit more like a Ferrari from the front. It's taking pride of place here, at Gooding & Company's Southern California showroom salon prior to its 2014 sale.*

Chapter 27

1971 Ferrari 365 GTB/4 Daytona Berlinetta

THE DISCO DAYTONA BREAKS COVER TO DANCE AGAIN

All photos by Darin Schnabel ©2015, courtesy RM Sotheby's and Kirk Gerbracht.

Few would question that the 365 GTB/4 Daytona is among the most desirable cars ever produced by Ferrari, and indeed one of the best performing and highly sought after exotics of the 1960s and 1970s. At the time, it was seen as a statement by Enzo Ferrari, who had yet to fully warm to the notion of "exotic" mid-engine high-performance grand touring models for the street. Of course, by the time the Daytona came to market in 1968, Ferrari had built, sold, and raced a variety of mid-engine race cars; yet il Commendatore was still convinced that mid-engine cars were fine for the track, but not for the street. He is often quoted as saying that "the horse pulls the cart; the horse never pushes the cart."

Arch-rival Lamborghini had set the exotic car world ablaze with the creation of the fabulously exotic mid-engine Miura, but Signore Ferrari felt the old "horse-in-front-of-the-cart" philosophy still had merit and many miles yet to go. Pininfarina's supremely talented Leonardo Fioravanti designed the 365 GTB/4, followed by a long line of fabulous, high-performance, front-engine gran turismo coupes including the 250 SWB, the 250 GTO, and more recently, the long-nose, short-deck 275 GTB.

Beneath its long sculpted nose sat something new: a larger, double overhead cam, and ever more powerful V-12. The 365 designation, as with all Ferraris at the time, described the displacement, in cubic centimeters, of just one of its cylinders. Do the math and you come up with 4.4 liters, or more exactly, 4,390 cc. The "4" in its model designation represented the four-overhead-camshaft design that had two cams per cylinder bank, topped with a sextet of Weber carburetors.

The result was 352 ultra-smooth, symphonic-sounding horsepower with an equally considerable torque rating of approximately 318 ft-lbs, solid low-end grunt for a high-winding thoroughbred V-12. Apart from its muscularly elegant looks, the 365 GTB/4 had a lot going for it, including four-wheel disc brakes, a rear-mounted 5-speed manual transaxle (to improve weight balance), and a fully independent suspension.

At first, the car wasn't officially named Daytona, but soon picked up the nickname to commemorate Ferrari's 1-2-3 finish in the 24-hour endurance race in Florida in 1967. Insiders around the company began calling it the Daytona, and the name ultimately stuck. And it proved to be an appropriate name, for even though the Daytona

Above: *The Daytona shape will become older but will never grow tiring. It's a long-nosed muscular look that certainly inspired the Ferrari 550 Maranello, 599 Fiorano, and F12 Berlinetta models that followed it. Daytonas were available with either the Borrani knock-off wire wheels, as seen on this car, or a five-spoked Cromodora knock-off alloy design.*

Facing Page: *One of Pininfarina's greatest Ferrari shapes. The Daytona is elegant, balanced, and yet aggressive from any angle, particularly in coupe form. You will note the silver painted nose on this European spec model. Some early Daytonas wore a Plexiglas nose panel with quad headlamps behind clear Plexiglas covers, although that design was ultimately replaced with a metal nose panel and more conventional hideaway headlights. Many enthusiasts like the look of this earlier design, and thus paint the fronts of their Daytonas silver to resemble the Plexiglas pieces.*

wasn't designed or produced primarily as a competition car, the factory did develop and produce a handful of competizione Daytonas. The car developed a considerable reputation as a tough, fast, and brilliant endurance racer, having won its class in long-distance events including Le Mans, Sebring, and of course, the 24 Hours of Daytona.

At first, the 365 GTB/4 Daytona was produced only as a berlinetta (or coupe, "B" designation). The 365 GTS spyder (or convertible, and "S" designation) came along in 1971. Both were produced through the 1973 model year; 1,284 GTBs and 122 365 GTSs were built.

A European-specification Daytona, picked up at the factory in 1971, chassis 14385 GT, was among them. Barn finds and lost cars are often the stuff of urban legend, sometimes true, sometimes not.

A Brand-New Daytona

According to RM Sotheby's, which consigned the Daytona for sale at its Amelia Island auction in March 2015: "The story told here belongs to one such legend, which has become known as the 'Condo-Find Daytona' or, thanks to the 8-track tape of disco rock still stuck in its K-Tec player, 'the Disco Daytona.'

"For the past 25 years, it has been hidden in plain sight, tucked away in the corner of a parking garage in downtown Toronto, where it has been up on blocks and under a cover, with –35 degree F antifreeze in its radiator. It is offered for sale at auction directly by its first and only owner, Patrick Sinn of Toronto. As is often the case with someone who has owned a car since new (44 years in this case), he tells the incredible story best:

"The year was 1971. I had just finished skiing in Chamonix, France, and I went to Geneva to catch a flight home. I was waiting in the airport for the flight to take off, and it was delayed, so I had the whole day to stand in the airport doing nothing. I heard about the Geneva International Motor Show, so I said, 'Why don't I just go there and check out the new models?'

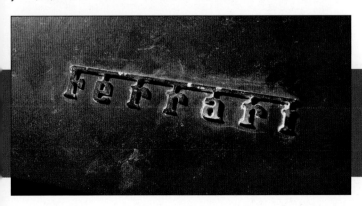

It's easy to see that, while not abused or stored outside, this Daytona hasn't seen wax or chrome polish in decades. Original metallic red/bronze is a beautiful color and will shine up handsomely at the hands of a good paint-detailing expert.

Left: *This wonderfully dated 8-track cassette tells you why this car is nicknamed the "Disco Daytona."* **Middle:** *Because this car was produced for international markets, not for North America, the speedometer and odometer are calibrated in kilometers not miles. Road & Track magazine considered the Daytona one of the ten best cars in the world for 1971. It had a true 175-mph top speed, and 0-60 in less than 6 seconds; both very quick for the day, and still are.* **Right:** *The engine runs well but is caked with crud; a serious underhood detail is in order here.*

"When I got there, Ferrari had a display of two Daytonas and a Dino 246. That was the first time I set eyes on the Daytona, and I fell in love with it. I sat in the car, walked around it a million times, and then said to myself, 'I want to buy one.'

"So I talked to the salesman at the motor show and asked him, 'How can I buy the Daytona?'

"He said, 'Well, you can go to any Ferrari dealership and place an order.'

"I said, 'Well, since I'm in Europe, I'm not going to wait. I'm going to go to the factory and just order a car and that way I can pick the color, options, and so on.'

"So, instead of flying home from Geneva to Toronto, I canceled my flight and bought a ticket to Milan. When I got off at the Milan airport, I rented a car and drove it all the way to Maranello, where the Ferrari office is. I went into the office and told the gentleman inside that I wanted to buy a Daytona.

"He introduced me to the sales manager, Mr. Boni, who showed me the list price, options, choice of color, and upholstery. I signed a contract to buy a Daytona and picked Bordeaux Red with a metallic base and the two-color upholstery that I like. They told me I had to come back in the summer, when the car was ready.

"I told them, 'I want to come here, take the car out of the factory, and drive it in Europe for a while before shipping it back.'

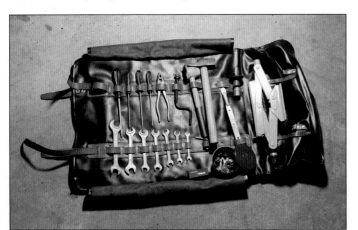

Left: *The factory tools, tool roll, and spare parts are intact and with the car as they should be. That's a lucky break for the next owner; replacing all this with the correct, factory bits for a Daytona would cost several thousand dollars.* **Right:** *Equally significant is the presence of the factory pack of books, manuals, and service records that came with the car. This is further evidence of its history.*

"They said, 'Fine. We will fit you with an EE license plate so you can drive it anywhere in Europe.'

"Approximately $18,000 later, plus a little more for spare parts tune-ups, and brake work, I gave Ferrari a deposit.

"In July 1971, they told me that the car was ready, so I flew over to Milan and got down to the factory and took possession of the new Daytona.

"When I first drove from the factory to Geneva, almost all the way on the autostrada, I stayed at the Inter-Continental Hotel in Geneva. While relaxing poolside, I was showered with admiration from strangers from all over Europe, wanting to talk with me about the shiny Daytona. It appeared to me that Europeans, in general, knew more about Ferraris than North Americans. I quickly made new friends around the pool. They wanted a ride in my car, and in return, they showed me around town, took me to restaurants and discotheques, and we all had a good time enjoying our new friendship. After that, I drove on the autobahn to Zurich and received a wonderful reception at the Dolder Grand Hotel.

"After Europe, and about a month of driving, I left the car at the factory for them to do the first oil change and check the engine over before they shipped it to North America. I drove it south to Marseilles, where I was catching the *QE2*, to sail from Marseilles to New York. They let me put the car on the ship and store it below deck, so that when I got off in New York, I could drive it home to Toronto. Every couple of days, I went below to look at the Ferrari, just to make sure there was no seawater damage!

"Of course, they told me at the U.S.–Canadian border that I could not import this car into Canada, because it did not meet all the safety and pollution requirements of a foreign import. I tried to convince them it was a one-off and not really causing any environmental damage, and

Equally elegant from the rear view, the Daytona was ultimately replaced by the 365 BB and 512 BB (boxer berlinetta) mid-engine coupe that Enzo Ferrari was so reluctant to green-light at the time the Daytona was being developed.

Leonardo Fioravanti, while at Pininfarina, was responsible for so many important Ferrari designs, from this great front-engine gran turismo, to the smaller, more modern, and strong selling mid-engine 308/328 that arrived a few years after the Daytona.

after haggling with them for a while, they just let me go, although I had to put up some kind of bond to clear customs. I guess in those days, 1971, there weren't too many foreign imports, and certainly not enough for them to worry about.

"In 1989, my dad passed away, and I had to rush to Hong Kong to take over his shipping business with my two brothers. Because I had to leave in a hurry, I just put the car up on blocks, covered it, and left, thinking, 'I'll be back in a few months.' But things didn't work out that way, because after the funeral, there were lots of estate matters to be resolved, so I ended up staying in Hong Kong for the next six years. I finally got back to Toronto, where I was heavily involved in real estate and extremely busy. I already had a Mercedes-Benz 280 SL and a Ford to drive, so I didn't need to drive the Ferrari.

"After a while, while looking at the car sitting in my garage, where they wash down the floors four times a year, I noticed that it was beginning to lose its shine. I

had two choices: I could spend big money to restore it, or I could sell my beloved toy and let somebody else enjoy it. I opted for the latter, realizing that, at 77 years old, I would not be enjoying the car as much as I used to, because I now had other priorities in life. So why not let another Ferrari aficionado enjoy it?"

RM Sotheby's continued, "The car has been returned to running condition but will require additional mechanical reconditioning before extensive road use. It was presented at the auction with its complete tool set, manuals, and incredible documentation. Offered on behalf of the original owner, including the 8-track disco rock cassette still lodged in the console-mounted tape deck."

This fabulous Daytona shows reasonable mileage, just 93,594 original kilometers (57,535 miles), which is not a lot for a car that is more than 40 years old. Considering that Daytonas have ridden the recent tidal wave of Ferrari V-12 price appreciation, with prime examples regularly now selling for more than $1 million, RM's initial sales price estimate of $600,000 to $750,000 didn't seem unreasonable.

It was easily among the most popular and attention grabbing lots at the company's Amelia Island auction on March 14, 2015, for a total, including all fees and commissions, of $770,000.

This car has certainly suffered a few nicks and battle scars along the way, but enough of the original paint remains, and is in undamaged condition. This car could be professionally touched up, rubbed out, and detailed to make it glow.

Above Left: *The 4.4-liter Ferrari quad cam V-12 is a big hunk of engine, taking up a lot of space in the Daytona's long nose. This one may be dirty, but it runs well and is likely good for many more miles before an expensive, but necessary, complete rebuild. Six thirsty Weber carbs sit underneath that long, stamped sheet-metal air box and produce a wonderful, vacuum cleaner–like roar when the Daytona's throttle is flat to the floor.* **Above Right:** *The original "Daytona pattern" red and black leather interior is intact. Although it is dusty and thirsting for leather conditioner, it can very likely be cleaned, treated, and saved without the need for a complete restoration.* **Below:** *Out of the garage and into the sun for the first time in nearly three decades. The now running but still dusty Daytona was among the stars of RM/Sotheby's March 2015 Amelia Island auction, selling for what many consider to be a reasonable $770,000. A $100,000 investment of paint touch ups and servicing, deep cleaning, and detailing will bring this car a very long way toward looking like a pampered original, many of which regularly sell for around $1 million at the time of this writing. (Photo courtesy of Kirk Gerbracht)*

Chapter 28

1972 Citroën SM

HOW DO YOU MIX FRENCH AND ITALIAN CUISINE? SIMPLE: PUT A MASERATI ENGINE IN A CITROËN

All photos courtesy of Stewart Reed and Matt Stone.

The Citroën SM of 1970–1975 is a fascinating automobile. Its unusual mix of avant garde French design and beautifully trimmed interior as well as complex hydraulic brake, suspension, and steering systems, plus front-wheel drive and an exotic Maserati V-6 engine make it appealing, and yet foreboding, on many levels. It's a mechanically complex but brilliant machine, elegant in style and design, beautiful to drive, and difficult to work on. This smorgasbord of unusual trait blending, for some reason, makes it particularly appealing to engineers, designers, and college professors.

Say "Citroën" and the image that comes to most minds is the "tin snail" 2CV "people's car" or the aerodynamically daring DS of the 1950s, 1960s, and 1970s. By the late 1960s, Citroën knew it needed to cap its model lineup with something even more dramatic than the decades old DS sedan. A 4-cylinder engine of one stripe or another always powered the DS, and the factory never offered it in any style other than a closed two-door coupe. Citroën management felt that a grand touring coupe powered by something more than a four-banger was in order, and set about designing its grand routier, or grand tourer, accordingly.

The French (and Italian) Connection

The company had plenty of design talent on hand for such a project, but no engine for it. The company cast about for an engine supplier/partner, and ultimately came to Maserati's doorstep in Modena, Italy. Maserati had many talents, but chief among them was that they knew how to design and engineer exotic power. However, the company's successful straight-6 engine was too long to practically engineer into a front-wheel-drive coupe and the big dual overhead cam V-8 was also too large and heavy.

Above: *You may wonder if Maserati developed the SM's V-6 for Citroën only, and the answer is no. Maserati put its first, new, modern engine to good use in its own "junior exotic," the Merak. This whimsical photo shows the same engine and transaxle installed in two very different cars. In the Citroën, it's installed "backward" with the transaxle in front, powering the front wheels. In the Merak SS, it's installed amidships with the transaxle in back, powering the rear wheels.*

Facing Page: *A far-more-than-average car sat sleeping in this otherwise average Southern California suburban two-car garage. (Sharp eyes don't miss the equally compelling original Studebaker Avanti parked next to it.) The SM's long and expansive hood opens for the first time in decades to reveal the car's Maserati-designed and -built 90-degree V-6. The green-painted metal "spheres" are accumulators for the car's high-pressure multi-function hydraulic system. Note the air-conditioner compressor; air conditioning was an absolute marketing must for luxury cars destined for the U.S. market.*

It was decided that a freshly designed, modern V-6 of approximately 3.0 liters would do the job for Citroën, and ultimately be of use to Maserati in its own cars. Citroën brought considerable global purchasing and distribution power to Maserati, and the Italian carbuilder had the pizzazz and high-performance engine building capabilities that Citroën required. so much so that Citroën ended up buying Maserati in its entirety in 1968.

The SM was developed primarily in France with Maserati providing 2.7- and 3.0-liter dual-overhead-cam (DOHC) V-6s to the project. The new car debuted in mid-1970, but production did not really amp up until the 1971 model year. Adding to the SM's considerable personality and engineering portfolio is a high-pressure hydraulic system used to regulate operation of the brakes, adjustable ride height suspension, and trigger-quick power assisted steering.

The ride was well controlled but cloudlike at the same time, and the 170-hp 2.7-liter Maserati V-6 provided ample power with a lusty growl. The car was a smash hit with the media, and sold well enough for several years. Most were powered by the 2.7, with the 3.0 joining line later in the model run. It was quite often backed with a 3-speed automatic transmission.

The French-Italian marriage wasn't the happiest of unions, and the market for relatively fuel-thirsty exotic cars wasn't so good in the early 1970s, so SM production wound down in 1975. Because of its many design and engineering advances, the SM played well in period road tests and European Car of the Year competitions.

Among the enthusiasts that gravitated toward the SM, Stewart Reed qualifies on two of those counts. He's an accomplished automotive designer, and is also a professor; he is the chairman of the Transportation Design program at the Art Center College of Design in Pasadena, California. Reed always has a stable of great cars in his garage, ranging from a Chip Foose–designed and built Pontiac Firebird to a pint-sized Fiat 600. He's had Porsches and Alfas, and is currently restoring another

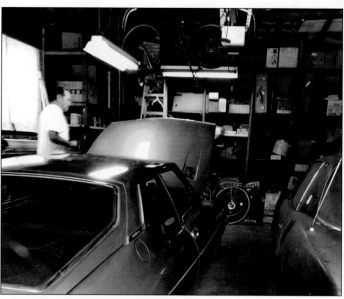

Left: *The SM's paint was a little faded when found, but the car was all there, down to its original, period-correct blue and yellow California license plates. The open headlight clusters also give this SM away as a North American–spec car; home-market Euro-spec cars had an innovative arrangement with three headlights per side. One of the lights swiveled in unison with the steering wheel, which provided an early 1970s example of today's turn-sensitive cornering lights.*
Right: *Shelving, bikes, stuff on the floor, plus a Citroën SM and an Avanti. SoCal's warm and dry weather certainly helped preserve both of these highly collectible cars, even though no over-the-top storage methods were employed.*

designer's favorite, a DeTomaso Mangusta. He also has a VW Beetle and an MG TC.

Time Capsule Revealed

In 2012, Reed was visiting the storied Autobooks–Aerobooks (one of the world's last great bookstores/news-stands dedicated solely to books and magazines about cars, motorcycles, and aircraft) in Burbank, California. The owner/manager, Tina Van Curren, handed him the phone and said, "Stewart, you need to talk to this guy."

Not knowing whom "this guy" was, Reed graciously took the phone and said hello. It turned out to be someone representing a family who had a Citroën SM they were interested in selling; it's no surprise that they called Autobooks, as Ms. Van Curren and her husband Chuck (an engineer) also own an SM.

The caller was representing the Veir family. Mr. Veir had bought a Citroën SM new from an Alhambra, California, dealership and the time had come to sell it. Veir had driven the car actively from its purchase until 1982–1983 when he suffered health issues that kept him from driving. At that time, he drove the elegant Fanco-Italo hybrid into his two-car garage in Pasadena, California, parked it, and never drove it again. The car was presented as being absolutely factory original and authentic in every way. The family was looking for a sympathetic enthusiast who would buy the car, return it to mechanical health, drive it, and enjoy it. Stewart Reed was just the man for the job.

This engine build plate gives the construction sequence, and further proof of its Maserati origin. V-6 engines were still relatively rare among European carmakers of the time, with only certain Lancias and Ferrari's Dino using them. The Maserati V-6 was an unusual design, in that its timing chain is mounted in the middle of the block, reaching up, between cylinder banks, to spin the cams. This powerplant was a good answer for the SM, however, with solid, smooth performance and plenty of prestige.

Left: Does this guy look happy or what? Designer and design educator Stewart Reed is obviously happy with his new barn find. Although much work and expense remained, Reed knew he'd found and acquired something extra special. **Middle:** The new license plate number CD 028 references the SM's landmark low co-efficient of drag (0.28). The license plate frame from the original, now defunct, selling dealer has been retained. **Right:** The attractive hood vent is actually a very stylish Citroën "double chevron" logo.

Above Left: Fortunately, the trunk included a small selection of books and manuals; great stuff when you find an old car. **Above Right:** The SM's original tan/gold/brown interior was dry and dusty but otherwise complete and in good condition. Only the scrubbing and leather treatment remains. **Below:** The long ride to a new home, out in the sunshine again for the first time since the early 1980s. The Veir SM says goodbye to South Pasadena on its way to the SM doctor's office, and subsequent return to the road.

Left: *New owner Reed's first "drive" in his new SM amounted to gently guiding it onto a flatbed for its trip to SM doctor Hathaway for mechanical ministrations and care. Reed wisely avoided the temptation to drop in a battery and restart the car; a stuck piston could have burned out the starter motor, stripped the starter ring gears, snapped a piston ring, or scored one or more of the cylinder walls.* **Right:** *Loaded and ready to ride toward its next life. The SM does not normally sit this low, but the hydraulic suspension had settled due to the engine not running for so many years. SM World took care of this with revitalized hydraulic "spheres" that pressurize the system to several hundred psi.*

After some discussions among Reed, the Veir family, and the family's representatives charged with selling the car, Reed paid a visit and was astounded at what he found. Opening the garage door revealed (in his words) "a time capsule" SM, looking very 1970s in its metallic gold paint, with yet another car designer's favorite, a Studebaker Avanti, sitting next to it. No mention was made of the Avanti's status or future, but Reed zoomed in on the glowing Citroën, marveling at its great condition and originality.

After inspection and investigation, he knew he had to have it. The car was resplendent in its slightly faded but original gold paint over a tan/brown interior. Because it was sold new in California, it was a proper American market spec car, with the 3.0-liter engine and automatic transmission. A brief negotiation ensued, and soon the car was his at a price fair to all parties.

The car hadn't run in some 30 years, so Reed made arrangements to have it trucked on a flatbed to nearby SM World, where Jerry Hathaway is acknowledged as the premier Citroën SM expert in the United States, and one of the best authorities on them in the world. Hathaway determined that the car was very original and in generally good stead, with less than 70,000 miles on the odometer. However, it was in need of a deep, thorough service and mechanical recommissioning.

Attempts to turn the engine over by hand indicated that it might have been seized or stuck due to its long

The SM is particularly dramatic and well proportioned in profile. This look leaves no doubt that the SM could be anything but a Citroën, and also gives some hints as to its aerodynamic efficiency. A few SMs wore a rare alloy wheel design, but most were equipped with steel wheels and these stainless steel hubcaps.

  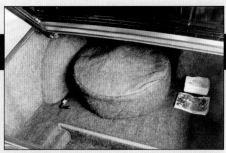

Left: *Citroën felt that the Maserati engine added considerably to the SM's prestige, so there was no attempt to create new cam covers that said "Citroën" or "Citroën Maserati." The factory simply retained the handsome cast-aluminum covers, the same covers found on the Maserati Merak.* **Middle:** *Reed's SM has yet to turn its 70,000th mile, although that day is coming soon. He notes that the Veir family drove it nearly every day during the 1970s, and is the veteran of several long-distance vacation drives.* **Right:** *The SM's trunk area required little other than a basic cleanup, and still carries the books, brochures, and service records that came with the car. Reed continues to gather and collect SM ephemera; he went to France to find some of it. It's all part of the fun of rescuing and enjoying a great exotic classic. The first aid kit is a good idea, and a fire extinguisher is a must for an older car with aged fuel lines; far too many great classic cars have been lost to fires that started small and could have been extinguished right away.*

hibernation. Hathaway pulled off the top half of the engine, and he and Reed agreed that the heads should be rebuilt; in fact, one of the cylinders was seized. After the engine and hydraulic system were serviced, all of the fluids were changed, and then the car was fired up for the first time in three decades.

The rest of the car needed a deep cleaning and show-level detail job to bring the paint and chrome back to a shiny luster; the interior leather and trim were reconditioned thoroughly. For this, Reed turned the car over to noted show car detail expert Bill Larzelere, who cleaned, waxed, and detailed every inch of the car's exterior, cabin, engine compartment, and chassis.

Seeing it today is like stepping back into 1972. The SM glows, yet retains that genuine mild patina of hon-esty and originality (glistening and immaculate) but not falsely shiny as it would be if disassembled and restored or refinished. Luckily, the storage conditions in which the car slept were kind, with no rust or animal infestation to destroy it. The car has since participated in countless local car shows, where it is always a favorite. It runs well, with the proud new owner driving it often.

This is a nearly perfect barn find story: a great car bought new by a loving and enthusiastic owner; lots of miles racked up during its first decade of every day use; a quiet, well protected 30-year nap; proper and sympathetic exhumation and revival; and a new proud, loving, and enthusiastic owner enjoying it again out on the road, where it belongs.

Left: *The SM's V-6 has been detailed for show, and the original quality is now sparkling from every corner. The air box caps a trio of Weber carburetors that give the engine good deep-breathing performance, and a wonderful intake roar when the throttle hits the floor.* **Right:** *The interior leather shows the mild patina of age, with some wear and modest cracking, but is original, and has held up reasonably well. Note the shifter quadrant for the rare Borg-Warner 3-speed automatic that was optional on the SM. Ovoid instruments are also an SM trademark, shared with the first-generation Meraks. Interior trimmings are high quality, in keeping with an expensive, European grand tourer.*

Chapter 29

1974 Dino 246 GTS

WHEN YOU DIG A HOLE THIS LARGE, BUILD A SWIMMING POOL, PLEASE!

We know that people often store great cars in damp, drafty barns, garages, or carports; it's the very foundation of this book. Smart, well-planned and properly executed long-term storage of a great car is one thing. Sticking it away with no thought to its protection, condition, or future is another.

But imagine digging a hole the size of a small swimming pool, lowering a [Ferrari] Dino into it, then covering it with dirt. Unthinkable, right? Yet somebody thought of it, and then actually did it. Buried cars are nothing new. And even being buried in a car isn't particularly novel, as many folks have chosen this path to interment.

When is a Ferrari not a Ferrari?

The fabulous Dino was originally intended as, for lack of a better term, a "junior sub-brand" of Ferrari. Named after Enzo Ferrari's eldest son, Alfredino (Dino for short), it also commemorated the fabulous V-6 engine that he helped to design and create. This engine was henceforth known as the Dino V-6. It was originally conceived as a racing engine (earning the Formula 1 championship in 1961 among other notable racing success), but street versions found their way into a pair of Fiat sports cars, appropriately named Fiat Dinos. Ferrari produced some Dino sports racers, and finally a street sports car called the Dino 246. At the time, they were not badged as full-fledged Ferraris because Enzo Ferrari decreed that, "a Ferrari is powered by a 12-cylinder engine."

After the run of Dino sports racers and some design concepts, the decision was made to put this "junior" Ferrari into series production. The design house of Pininfarina, Ferrari's favorite at the time, whipped up a dandy mid-engine coupe for production. The model began in 1969 as the road-going Dino, called the 246 GTB (gran turismo berlinetta, or coupe). It was an absolute jewel to behold.

Curvaceous and sensuous, the Dino was powered by a 2.4-liter version of the Dino V-6, mounted amidships, with a 5-speed transaxle. The car wasn't crazy fast but still plenty quick; magazine road testers of the day often compared it to the contemporary Porsche 911S.

It wasn't long before demand grew for an open-topped version of the car, and Pininfarina's reply was appropriate, logical, and just as beautiful. It was called the 246 GTS (gran turismo spyder, or convertible), although its convertible top wasn't of the conventional folding variety. Instead, it had a removable roof section, much like the competing Porsche Targa. Reconfiguring the Dino for a conventional folding top would have meant a major redesign because the top would have to fold into a spot just aft of the seats, currently occupied by the V-6 engine. This made no sense for such a low-volume automobile. Instead, the pullout targa roof panel left sail panels, a rear window, and a pair of buttresses aft of the seats.

The GTB was produced from model year 1969 to 1974, while the open GTS was produced from 1972 to 1974 only. A total of 3,761 Dinos were built; of them 1,274 were the more rare, and ultimately more desirable, GTS model. In U.S.–spec form, the GTS's V-6 was good for 175 hp.

At the beginning, the Dino wore only Dino badging; many didn't consider it a "true Ferrari." Time has softened that stance considerably, and now nearly everyone properly considers it a "Ferrari Dino."

The Lost Dino

Dino 07865 GTS was born as a 1974 model, originally in a medium green color, wearing beautiful cast Campagnolo alloy wheels, subtly flared fenders, and "Daytona" style seat upholstery. This combination earned the nickname "chairs and flares" and added considerably to its desirability then and now, and certainly to its current potential collector value.

The car was sold new to a private owner in Beverly Hills. It was reported stolen from its parking spot in front of the famous Brown Derby restaurant in Los Angeles, where the owners were enjoying an anniversary dinner in late 1974. The Los Angeles Police Department opened an investigation into the theft. Bank of America was the lienholder; because the car was thought to be lost, Farmers Insurance paid off the $22,500 loan, and the car was written off as a total loss.

Even after considerable police and insurance investigation, the story gets murky. Did the original owner arrange to have the car "stolen," thereby planting the seeds for a major insurance fraud? Or was it actually stolen and then disposed of by thieves attempting to hide the evidence?

The story went dormant until 1978 when someone was digging around in a front yard in South Central Los Angeles when the shovel hit metal. The police were called, and the Ferrari was dug up to the shock and awe of countless onlookers. It was big news on Los Angeles television, and in local newspapers, for some time. The joke making the rounds at the time was, "Knock, knock." "Who's there?" "I want to buy a used Ferrari. Got any?" "No but I'll see what I can dig up."

There's little question that the car's undertakers planned to return to it, given some rudimentary attempts to protect it. Towels were stuffed into partially lowered windows, plastic was packed into the exhausts and carburetors, and so on. Nothing helped. The leather interior was rotted and ruined, the body and chrome pocked with rust. The car was considered a total loss, but what should be done with the dirty, damaged corpse?

After the car was pulled out of its grave, it was shipped to a warehouse in nearby Pasadena to be displayed for inspection and the solicitation of bids. Sadly, many more parts of the car disappeared during this process. Farmers didn't disclose the high bid for the car, but it is believed to have been between $5,000 and $9,000. A young mechanic from nearby Burbank reportedly bought the car with the intent to bring it back to life.

The car changed hands a few times after that, but has since been fully restored and is back to its former life and glory. It was a good call by someone along the way, as Dino GTSs routinely sell for hundreds of thousands of dollars. It currently wears the vanity license plate "DUGUP."

Facing Page: *It's a sight so crazy as to be nearly unimaginable. A beautiful and rare Ferrari 246 Dino GTS being dug up from burial in a South Los Angeles yard. The damage from dirt, moisture, and the passage of about four years underground initially suggested that the Dino was unrestorable. However, after its rescue, it was fully restored to beauty, health, and roadworthy condition. (Photo Copyright 1978* **Los Angeles Times,** *Larry Sharkey. Reprinted with Permission)*

Chapter 30

One Barn, Three Maserati Ghiblis, and an F5000/Can-Am Racer

IT'S A LONG WAY FROM MODENA, ITALY, TO MODESTO, CALIFORNIA; SO HOW DID WE GET HERE?

All photos courtesy of Daniel Rapley.

By any measure, the original Maserati Ghibli coupe of 1967–1973 is an all-time great Italian exotic gran turismo. Beautiful almost to a fault, the Ghibli is the masterwork of Giorgetto Giugiaro, who some credit as the most accomplished and greatest-ever automotive designer. Giugiaro designed countless exotic cars and many seminal basic transportation boxes, including the original Fiat Panda, and Volkswagen's first water-cooled production car, the original mid-1970s Golf (Rabbit to U.S. consumers). Those designs, while boxy and basic, were perfectly realized for cars that were roomy and efficient for their size, easy to build and drive, and cost effective to produce and sell.

Giugiaro also designed many fabulous mid-engine exotics, production models, and one-off concept cars, including the gorgeous, if mechanically flawed, DeTomaso Mangusta, the later Maserati Bora and Merak, the Lotus Esprit, and the DeLorean DMC-12. In addition to his mid-engine design portfolio, there are many great front-engine GTs including the all-time-favorite Alfa Romeo GTV, the Corvette-powered Gordon-Keeble, a majority of the Iso Rivolta lineup, and the Maserati Ghibli, first shown in 1966 and first available on the market as a 1967 model.

Giugiaro did stints at several of Italy's most well known design houses, including Bertone and Ghia, prior to striking out on his own in the late 1960s to form ItalDesign in Turin. Born in August 1938, Giugiaro was later joined in the family business by his son Fabrizio. The

Above: *This silver example is chassis number 210, wearing proper Maserati-spec alloy wheels. This car is much more representative of what later "production" Ghiblis looked like in terms of specification, trim, switchgear, chrome, badging, etc. This is Giugiaro design at its considerable best.*

Facing Page: *It's difficult to confirm the original colors of this vehicle, the fourth Maserati Ghibli produced. Its handsome Giugiaro coachwork is covered in an aged combination of primer and body filler. Regardless, it's a sight that'll stir the heart of any serious barn finder.*

Below: *Ghibli chassis number 088 is theoretically the 44th Ghibli produced in late 1967 or early 1968. It appears to have worn this metallic maroon paint scheme since birth, although these Cromodora five-spoke alloy wheels are completely wrong for this car. They are the wheels and design most often seen on the Ghibli's arch competitor, Ferrari's 365 GTB/4 Daytona, as well as some Alfa Romeos.*

Left: *Here, Ghibli 210 has been moved to a different location, has had its tires pumped up, and has been washed; it definitely looks snappier than it did packed away in the barn. The grille surround, mesh, and headlights appear to be missing, but the rather dull silver paint shows off its lines and curves. You'll have to look very hard to find a more elegantly masculine Italian GT than the Ghibli. Vehicle designers love silver, and what it does for nearly any set of shapes; this is one of the reasons that so many show cars, concept cars, and design studies are painted silver.* **Right:** *Not even Clark Gable or Cary Grant had a stronger profile than did the Ghibli coupe. The windowline is elegant with relatively slim A-pillars, and evokes speed and aerodynamics. Side vents in the front fenders are functional, allowing engine heat air to exit the engine compartment. This photo was taken after a quick clean-up at the barn in Modesto.*

father-son team designed many more great cars, before selling the majority of their business to Volkswagen.

The original front-engine Ghibli coupe was fashioned on a tubular steel frame with a separate body structure. It was only ever powered by a street version of Maserati's successful racing-derived all-aluminum double overhead cam V-8; no straight-6s, V-6s, or V-12s for the Ghibli. Over time, the engines available were 4.7 and 4.9 liters in displacement, with horsepower ranging from 310 to 330. A rare and ultra-handsome convertible, the Ghibli Spyder, ultimately joined the lineup; in all, 1,170 coupes and 125 spyders were produced. In 1973, the Ghibli went out of production; the Bertone-designed Maserati Khamsin replaced it the following year.

The Ghibli's competition included the Ferrari 365 GTB/4 Daytona; the Lamborghini Islero and Jarama, and to some extent the 2+2 Espada; the Iso Rivolta and Grifo; and to some eyes, even top-level versions of the Chevrolet Corvette. The Ghibli was the darling of the moneyed jet set; a searingly beautiful machine that was fast and handled well, but was more directly aimed at high-speed, long-legged grand touring than racetrack-style corner carving. Movie stars, musicians, captains of industry, and seemingly half of the population of Monaco bought them.

Left: *Chassis 008 appears to have suffered the most from its time in the barn; it was parked on dirt and likely wasn't in cosmetically great condition when it was stored. There's no information as to why the car was stripped of paint and covered in body filler. Maybe it was to either prep it for a repaint or protect the body from further deterioration. Still, it's a remarkably complete car for such an early example. It certainly deserves a platinum-level concours restoration from the ground up.* **Middle:** *Even though 008 has suffered rust and storage damage, it's remarkably complete, which will make its restoration at least straightforward, if not easy or inexpensive. You have to love the mechanic in his very Italian, light blue mechanic's jumpsuit, which is not so different from what the assembly workers in Modena likely wore when building this car in the late 1960s.* **Right:** *It looks as if 008 suffered minor accident or body damage at some point because the rust, primer, and paint on this fender don't match the layer of body filler troweled onto the rest of the car. Poor baby! Note the missing door handle and lock assembly.*

On the surface, Ghibli 210 appears to be in the best condition of the three. All of its rear-end trim, lights, bumpers, and exhaust are intact. You can see the tip of the right rear of the silver car just visible in the lower left-hand corner. Fortunately these cars were parked on cement, a good surface for long-term storage. A dirt floor, on the other hand, soaks up moisture when cold and bleeds out moisture when warm. Also, mold doesn't grow on dry concrete with the same enthusiasm that it does on damp, soft, dirt.

Ghiblis A-Plenty in the Barn

Ghiblis were built in Maserati's longstanding factory in Modena, Italy, and sold in many world markets, including the United States. *Somehow*, three very early production Ghiblis ended up stored in a barn in Modesto, a central California agricultural town. Keep in mind that this is a town more populated by John Deere tractors and Chevy pickup trucks than designer Maseratis. And equally *somehow*, Connecticut-based Daniel Rapley found them.

Each individual of this Ghibli trio is distinctly different in small ways, common with early production examples. The designs and components employed tended to evolve quickly as production ramped up, a phenomena particularly true of low-volume Italian cars of the 1950s, 1960s, and 1970s.

On these pages, the tan-colored Ghibli is chassis number 008, the maroon vehicle is car number 088, and the silver Maserati is chassis 210. Using the Ghibli's "even numbered" chassis sequencing system these are the 4th, 44th, and 105th Ghiblis produced.

Rapley tells his story: "I had been talking with a man in Modesto regarding his Ghiblis. He had restored several others and these three unrestored cars remained. I flew in and inspected them. They had been sitting in a pigeon-infested barn for many years and possums had been living in the engine compartments. The interiors were dirty and crawling with spiders. The cars were a challenging sight.

Left: All three Ghiblis were stored with their VIN and dataplates intact and in good condition. TIPO: AM 115 means "Type: Alfieri Maserati Ghibli" and of course 088 is the individual chassis number. As Ghiblis were "even numbered," this suggests that chassis 088 is the 44th car produced in the model run. **Middle:** The 088's engine compartment appears relatively complete and largely undamaged. Someone at least tried some minimal preservation efforts by stuffing plastic between the radiator and the front grille surface. The fact that the original air filter housing is still intact certainly helped protect the Weber carbs and the aluminum intake manifold. Note the quartet of air horns mounted to the inner fenderwell. These Trident air horns are typical of many Maserati models, powered by a tiny air compressor that blasted the horn when the driver pressed the horn button inside. **Right:** Lots of rat families partied hearty on the maroon car's interior, although it's generally complete including all of the instrumentation, switchgear, and rare expensive aluminum/wood steering wheel. This car has a manual transmission. Maserati also offered the car with a 3-speed automatic as an option, which doesn't sound terribly sexy or sporty. However, it actually complemented the car's easy-to-drive, grand-touring nature, and worked pretty well given the V-8's solid low-end torque output.

Left: *The silver car's interior appears to be in reasonably good condition, with little bug or rodent infestation. It'll still be a fair amount of work to put this cabin really right, but all the pieces are there with what appears to be minimal deterioration and damage. The odometer reading is not clear in this photo, but it can't be too high given the minimal wear on the seats and other upholstery.* **Middle:** *It's difficult to know when or why the early 008 gave up much of its switchgear and instrumentation, but putting this one right will be difficult and expensive. It is also likely that the pieces from a later Ghibli might not fit or look proper in this early example, but the next owner or restorer may have little choice but to retrofit the closest-fitting parts that can be located.* **Right:** *This rust damage didn't likely occur while the red car was parked in the barn, it appears to be pre-existing damage. It's not uncommon on these cars; factory rustproofing was marginal at best. It'll take some work and skill, but this damage is easily repairable. Given that the Ghibli uses separate frame and body structures, this isn't likely structural.*

"I made an offer on the three cars and he turned me down. So I made an offer on two of them. Still he turned me down. Then I asked about the fourth car, which was under a cover. It was a single seater Can-Am racer. Still no deal. So I left.

"About a week later we were able to settle on a number for all four cars and I flew back to pull them out of the barn and clean them as best I could. These photos show the cars as found, and coming out of the barn.

"The Ghiblis were what I expected. The Can-Am car was not. It was, in fact, an old Lola F5000 T332, converted and bodied to run in the mid- to late-1970s Can-Am. It was the car in which Brian Redman won the F5000 championship. I forget if it was from 1974 or 1975. The car came with a logbook from its Can-Am days. It had been chopped and changed but was the real deal. After cleaning and photographing, I sold some and kept some.

"Isn't it great that they are still lurking out there in dirty old barns?"

Rapley did a considerable amount of research on his three Maseratis' chassis numbers. He believes that 008, early in its life, belonged to Henry Ford II. He was Henry Ford's eldest grandson, a longtime president of the Ford Motor Company, and loved all things Italian; his second wife was Italian and he owned a home in Italy.

In the early 1960s, while at the helm of Ford, he attempted to orchestrate the company's acquisition of Ferrari. That transaction was all but finalized when Enzo Ferrari realized that, for the operation of his most beloved Formula 1 racing team, he'd have to be appealing to Dearborn for the approval of certain decisions and expenditures, and it was about that time that the deal blew up.

Henry Ford, however, ended up adding several significant Italian automotive entities to his portfolio, by the ultimate purchase of DeTomaso Automobili (in Modena, Italy); the Vignale body plant (also in Italy); and Ghia, the design house and coachbuilder. The notion of Henry

Even though the Ghibli looks like a "fastback hatchback" it is not; instead it's a proper coupe with a conventional trunk lid and cargo compartment. If you think you've seen these taillights before, it's likely you have; they've appeared on many Maserati models, as well on as most DeTomasos and a handful of Alfa Romeos.

Left: *Someone took measures to protect the silver car's engine; the intake trumpets of the four Weber carbs have been wrapped in what appears to be duct tape. Probably not as good as leaving the factory air filter and metal air filter housing in place (but better than nothing), and having an intake manifold full of bugs and rodent skeletons. Some of the engine's front-mounted accessories are missing. It will make for some extra work, but there won't be major difficulty finding the bits. Setting it all right shouldn't be too big a deal with the powertrain removed.* **Right:** *Lots of expensive chrome trim is missing from the front of the silver car, including the entire grille and bumper/grille surround, center Maserati Tridente insignia, and the running lights. But at least the headlights and headlight doors survived, making this tough job a little easier.*

Ford owning an early Ghibli comes as no surprise at all.

It appears that this car was found to be in the most compromised condition among the three Maseratis. Rapley continues: "This Ghibli had some problems. The chassis stamping looked correct and untouched, but the tail of the car was incorrect for this early a Ghibli. The early cars have a drop-down trunk lid and a tail to accommodate it. Everything else looked fine, except for the rust and incompleteness."

Rapley's not clear about whether he had planned to keep or restore one or more of the Ghiblis (or the Lola race car). However, he's since sold all three Maseratis; he didn't disclose what he paid for this great find, or how much he gained from the sale of it. Nevertheless, it's an outstanding story, and should give hope and fantasy to barn finders everywhere. It's great that you can still find something fabulous in an old dusty barn in the middle of the countryside.

Left: *Formula 5000 was an open-wheel racing series, so why is this Lola wearing this type of bodywork? As the F5000 series was ending in the mid-1970s, the Can-Am was reformulated as a series for primarily small-block V-8 cars. That made this Lola 332 the perfect candidate for some plastic surgery to become a full-bodied Can-Am racer. It looks like some of the original F5000–spec bodywork is sitting just behind the car.* **Right:** *Without the bodywork, the Lola chassis looks more like the formula car that it was when born. Assuming that all of the paperwork is correct, this car's provenance as an ex-Brian Redman machine is significant and of great value. Redman won the F5000 championship an unequalled four times, competing against the very best in the series: Mario Andretti, Al Unser, Bobby Unser, James Hunt, David Hobbs, Tony Adamowicz, Sam Posey, Ian Ashley, John Cannon, and Eppie Wietzes all raced in the series over time. Several of them are CART, USAC, Indy 500, and F1 champions.*

Chapter 31

60-Car Barn Find in France

JUST YOUR AVERAGE MULTI-ACRE FRENCH CHATEAU

All photos courtesy of Artcurial, ©2014.

Finding a great exotic car in a barn could be a life-changing experience. The uncovering and sale of 60 of them from a single collection in the southwest of France would certainly be worldwide news. And it was.

French industrialist Roger Baillon earned his post–World War II fortune in the heavy-duty trucking business. Among other pursuits, he chose to enjoy his success by living in a fine and luxuriously appointed chateau while assembling a world-class automobile collection. Baillon's tastes were varied and superb; as you might expect, he tended to favor the finest examples, often one-offs, of the great French marques, but his taste wasn't limited by his nationality or patriotism.

Spread about the carports and garages on his estates were, among many other vehicles, the odd Hispano-Suiza, several Ferraris, and a custom-bodied one-off of his own design and creation called the Oiseau Bleu, or Blue Bird, in addition to countless Delahayes, Delages, and Bugattis. Baillon was reputed to enjoy fettling and maintaining his own cars, but with the passage of time, many of the cars were parked outside in makeshift lean-tos, rusting, rotting, and otherwise going to seed. At one point, his collection numbered approximately 100 cars; his remaining family decided to auction off 60 of them, using the money to restore and maintain the rest to continue Baillon's legacy and love of the automobile.

The family chose Artcurial, France's premier auction company, to handle the sale of these five dozen cars. The group included examples from a handful of small, everyday compacts and production models to a rare, highly sought after, and certain to be expensive covered-headlight Ferrari 250 GT Spyder California. Some of the best cars were stored inside relatively dry buildings and garages, while others were stacked door to door, exposed to the elements and ranged in condition from average to poor to parts car.

When was the last time you saw an IRAT Cabriolet, the car at far left? I'm guessing never. The big four-door in the middle is a Facel Vega Excellence, a French-bodied high-performance executive sedan running Chrysler V-8 power.

The following is excerpted from The Artcurial Motorcars press release of May 12, 2014 announcing "The Discovery of the Baillon Collection: A Forgotten Treasure in France." It also announced that 60 of the 100 cars found would be auctioned on February 6, 2015 as part of the Paris Rétromobile Salon. Matthieu Lamoure, Managing Director of Artcurial Motorcars and Pierre Novikoff, senior specialist at Artcurial Motorcars discuss, with obvious passion, how the collection was discovered, and what it means to the automotive community.

It was in the West of France that the team from Artcurial's collectors' car department made an extraordinary discovery. Forgotten for almost 50 years, some 60 automobiles assembled with devotion to create a private museum that would pay tribute to this great human invention. Matthieu Lamoure and Pierre Novikoff, of Artcurial Motorcars, tell us about this incredible find.

Artcurial: This has been like finding real treasure. Is it something that happens often to you?

Matthieu Lamoure (ML), Managing Director of Artcurial Motorcars: This sort of thing doesn't happen often enough! I think, above all, you go into this profession for discoveries like this. Yes, this really is a treasure. No doubt a once-in-a-lifetime discovery. In our jargon, we speak about "barn finds" as cars that are intact, that have remained untouched for years, and are found again.

I have to say that when we arrived here, we found ourselves overcome with emotion. Probably much like Lord Carrington and Howard Carter, on being the first

Even though this rare and fabulous Frua Maserati was overshadowed by the Ferrari California parked next to it, the Maserati is a special piece all on its own, and on that day in France, it brought $2.2 million.

Facing Page: Given that the Baillon chateau estate encompasses several acres of property, someone surely could have found a better place than the hood of a rare and exceedingly valuable Ferrari 250 GT Spyder California upon which to stack a thousand pounds of old magazines and newspapers. Just imagine yourself as a barn finder, opening this garage door and finding the rare Ferrari inside, plus this Frua-bodied Maserati A6GS coupe. What a great spot to have your heart attack, no?

It's possible that this tile-roofed open storage structure was built to house these cars, but it is more likely that its original use was as a stable. The cars lost, found, and sold range from the average to the astounding. Note rear-end-damaged Ferrari Mondial cab at far right.

people for centuries to enter Tutankhamen's tomb. It really was a case of waking up Sleeping Beauty.

Pierre Novikoff (PN), senior specialist at Artcurial Motorcars: We are treasure hunters! I don't think that the collectors' car world has seen anything like this since the Schlumpf Collection. This is surely the last time that such a discovery will be made, anywhere in the world. What is so special here is the number of cars (60), the range (from the early days of the motor car to the 1970s), the quality, and pedigree of the models. Unlike the Schlumpf collection that was known about and documented, ours is completely new. It's a discovery!

Artcurial: This is becoming a specialty!

ML: I must say that at Artcurial Motorcars, we are committed to finding cars that have rarely or never been seen on the market before. This is our signature style, and it requires an incredible amount of work. We spend the year crossing Europe and travelling around the world. It is no coincidence that collectors come to our sales from across the globe year after year. In 2014, we realized close to €50 million [$66 million] in sales, which is up 67 percent on 2013.

PN: The prices and the records are a welcome reward for our hard work. But to arrive in a small village in the West of France, and discover this treasure, is unheard of."

Artcurial: How, exactly, did this start?

PN: It is quite a story. A key part of our profession is being able to build relationships and to listen when we are told about something. On that particular day, I had a feeling that something was going to happen. On the phone, I gathered from the information I was given, that this could turn out to be something important. Without realizing the scale. I spoke to Matthieu immediately and we arranged to go there, to find out what it was.

Artcurial: And when you arrived, what happened?

ML: It was a fairly indescribable feeling. On entering the gates of this property, we had no idea what we would find. We had to go in through the gardens at the rear of the property, to get a first look. Across three hectares [approximately seven acres], we could see different makeshift structures. Low shelters covered with corrugated iron. From there, we realized that this was something big. We still didn't know what we were looking at, but could make out coachwork, weathered by time and the elements. Some modern shapes and others that were older.

PN: Incredible! The cars weren't stored in solid, purpose-built sheds, but in completely makeshift constructions. We came closer and realized that there were dozens of cars parked underneath. We soon realized that some of these had been put there 50 years earlier and left untouched. Wooden posts, between the cars supported the fragile roofs. The sides were open to the elements. We still didn't realize exactly what we were faced with: the number of cars, the marques, or their condition.

Artcurial: It was practically an archeological excavation you were looking at!

ML: Exactly! However, before the inventory, recording, and researching their history, we needed to see everything. We continued our exploration at a second site, at the bottom of a field, then in one of the property's outbuildings, an old barn that had been converted into an improvised garage.

PN: The artistic and aesthetic shock first of all, faced with the beauty of these metallic sculptures. The emotional shock followed, as we came across incredible models and iconic marques. This was somewhere between a metallic graveyard and a museum. Nature had taken a hold, over

Left: *Among the many prized French cars in the collection, and sold by Artcurial at its Rétromobile sale is this Saout-chik-bodied Talbot Lago T26 Grand Sport coupé. It was another strong seller. Despite its rundown condition and collapsed roof, it brought $1.9 million.* **Right:** *Another fine bit of French autocraft, this Chapron-bodied 1952 Delahaye 235 coupe is in much better and more complete condition than this photo indicates. It was judged by some experts as a minor bargain at $76,592.*

the years. Ivy had invaded a car and entirely covered its wheel, while weeds had taken root in a passenger compartment as easily as in a greenhouse. In places, the sheets of corrugated iron were resting directly on the cars.

Artcurial: But what is the story behind this treasure?

ML: Of course, this is the first question we asked ourselves! In front of such a collection, how could we not be curious, and want to find out? How had someone been able to amass so many cars? And for what purpose?

PN: Little by little, thanks to the owners, we learned the story and the pieces of the puzzle began to fall into place. We were standing in front of the Baillon collection. Well documented, it had given rise to a large sale during the 1970s. It was thought that everything had been sold, and its existence had been forgotten about. And here, we had just found the lost collection! The troupe of red lorries [trucks], associated with the celebrated Transports Baillon [company] in the mid-20th century, left us in no doubt.

Artcurial: How did it come to be lost?

PN: I must tell you the story! It is essentially that of a great inventor and automobile enthusiast, although the collection was put together over several generations. Until 1977, Roger Baillon had a transport and truck manufacturing business in the west of France. In 1947, this guy, who was crazy about machines, made a name for himself. He exhibited a car he had designed himself: the Oiseau Bleu [blue bird]. It was an ingenious vehicle, sculptural. It was the work of an artist, built to the highest standards.

ML: Roger Baillon made his fortune manufacturing trucks, at a time when the transport business was booming, after the war. He had the monopoly on [building] transports for dangerous liquid chemicals, thanks to the design of a secure, watertight tank. At the same time, he produced a revolutionary lorry in 1950 that featured the first "cabine avancée" [forward-control cab] in the transport industry! It was moving to find the relics of this great era in the garden of the property.

PN: It was between 1955 and 1965 that he amassed the largest part of the models. Unfortunately, during the 1970s, he suffered a reverse of fortune and his business went into decline. Which explains the large sale at the end of that decade.

Artcurial: But why collect the cars?

PN: This needs to be put into context. Although collectors' cars, particularly post-war French models, are snapped up today in the salerooms, this has not always been the case. At that time, Roger Baillon saved many of these cars from the scrapyard. With many significant models amongst them!

ML: This man was one of the early collectors. He wanted to celebrate the art of automotive engineering and bought a property to turn into an automobile museum. He began to buy key models in France and Europe. Having a transport business, it was straightforward for him to have his treasure delivered to the property he had bought in 1953 for this purpose. He even acquired a little train, which he planned to use to make a tour of the museum that would pass by all the cars.

PN: When the vehicles arrived, he put them away without much fuss, one next to the other. He restored some and left others as they were. He passed on his passion to his children and grandchildren. They continue to be very attached to this collection that they had watched expand, with the cars they had grown up around.

Artcurial: I imagine that you went from one discovery to another when you started to make an inventory?

ML: Sixty cars, legendary marques, in "barn find" condition. It was already unbelievable! We had already spotted a few gems during our first tour of the machines, and making an inventory made us start to comprehend the extent of the collection. One mythical coachbuilder after another. I must tell you about three Talbots designed by Saoutchik: Despite their condition, it was impossible not to fall in love with the lines of the Talbot Lago T26 Record coupé by Saoutchik. It is like a work of art by Brancusi. When we contacted the marque historian to tell him we had found this car, he couldn't believe it! Once he had recovered from the shock, he bombarded us with questions.

PN: I'm not sure I've ever seen so many exceptional cars together in one collection: Bugatti, Hispano-Suiza, Talbot-Lago, Panhard-Levassor, Maserati, Ferrari, Delahaye, and Delage. Roger Baillon saved these cars and succeeded in his task: to trace the history of the automobile through the finest examples! When I look at the imposing Hispano-Suiza H6B cabriolet Millon-Guiet, a car built in France, I am impressed by the attention to detail and its proportions. These men were genuine artists.

Artcurial: You speak of them like genuine works of art.

PN: But that's what they are! It is no coincidence that Artcurial has a collectors' car department. Certain cars, much like paintings or sculptures, are works of art, created by artists. Not only the engineering, but their styling reflects the history of design.

ML: I think you can feel the same emotion whether you are looking at the cubist forms of Pablo Picasso, the geometric but gentle shapes of Constantin Brancusi, a bookcase by the designer Ron Arad, or the perfect styling of a Ferrari 250 GT SWB California Spyder.

Artcurial: Tell me about this Ferrari. It is THE discovery?

ML: Only 37 examples of this model were built making it extremely rare. Every example has been carefully documented by historians and this one was thought to be lost. We have found it!

PN: And we really did "find" it. It was buried, in a garage, under a pile of papers (old copies of *La Vie de l'Auto*) and various covers. Not what you would expect for a car worth between €9.5 and €12 million [$12 and $16 million]. Its neighbor was another gem, a Maserati A6G Gran Sport Frua.

Artcurial: Do any of these cars have special history?

ML: The Ferrari, certainly! When we were making the inventory, we realized that the car used to belong to Alain Delon.

PN: It had been bought new by the actor Gérard Blain who sold it to his fellow actor Alain Delon. Delon was photographed several times at the wheel of this machine: in 1964 with Jane Fonda during the filming of *Les Félins* and on the Côte d'Azur with Shirley MacLaine.

ML: The collection also contains an extravagant Talbot Lago T26 cabriolet that once belonged to King Farouk.

Artcurial: What can you do with vehicles in this condition?

PN: All the cars are significant for their heritage, and we hope that some of them will join big collections in and outside France. Perhaps even museums. They will be displayed and sold as they are. Just as we found them. Possibly one or two spider's webs may be lost in transit, and some of the dust blown away, but that's all.

ML: What is incredible is the condition of these cars. I think some should be left as they are, and others should be restored. This is a unique testimony. It is the collectors who have this opportunity to make the successful bid who will decide. If you think about it, there are always restored cars available to buy on the market. These vehicles are unique. This is a very rare opportunity presenting works of art unknown to the market! As to the Talbot Lago T26 Grand Sport coupé Saoutchik, caved in at the rear, I think it should be left in this condition. It is a sculpture.

Artcurial: The cars will be on display during the salon Rétromobile, in February 2015. How do you transport such fragile objects?

ML: It is a highly technical and precise job, the same as transporting a work of art. We need to take as much care as if we were moving the *Mona Lisa*. The cars are loaded manually into special lorries [trucks], to be taken to a warehouse. There, like celebrities, they will be individually photographed in a studio, inspected and written up for the sale catalogue.

PN: You will see them again in February at the Parc des Expositions de la Porte de Versailles, in the major exhibition that precedes the sale on 6 February, at the Rétromobile Salon.

The comprehensive list of cars is mind-boggling:

Amilcar C6 berline	Avions Voisin limousine C15	Berliet Type VIGB 10HP Taxi
Amilcar CGS	Avions Voisin C7 par Gallé	Landaulet
Ariès coach	Ballot 8-cylinder limousine	Bugatti 57 Ventoux
Auto Union cabriolet	Barré torpédo	Citroën Trèfle
Avions Voisin C15	Berliet coupé chauffeur	Delage D6

Delage D8 coach
Delahaye 135 cabriolet Faget Varnet
Delahaye 135 coach Chapron
Delahaye 235 coach Chapron
Delahaye 235 coach Chapron
Delahaye 235 coupé Chapron
Delahaye Type 43 coupé chauffeur
Delahaye GFA 148 L
Delahaye Type 43 camionnette
Delaunay Belleville limousine VL8
Facel Vega Excellence
Ferrari 250 GT SWB California Spyder
Ferrari 308 GTS i
Ferrari 400
Ferrari Mondial 3.2L cabriolet
Hispano-Suiza H6B cabriolet
   Millon-Guiet

Hotchkiss cabriolet
Innocenti S cabriolet
Jaguar type S 3.4 L
La Buire 12 A
Lagonda LG45 cabriolet
Lancia Thema 8.32
Lorraine Dietrich B3/6 plateau
Lorraine Dietrich B3/6 torpédo par
   Grumman
Lorraine-Dietrich torpédo
Maserati A6G 2000 Gran Sport Frua
Mathis cabriolet
Mathis FOH
Packard cabriolet Super Eight
Panhard-Levassor Dynamic berline X77
Panhard-Levassor Dynamic coupé X76
Panhard-Levassor limousine X72

Porsche 356 SC ex-Sonauto
Renault AX torpédo
Renault Vivastella cabriolet
Sandford cyclecar 3 roues
Singer Cabriolet
Talbot Lago 11/6 cabriolet
Talbot Lago Baby cabriolet
Talbot Lago Baby cabriolet
Talbot Lago Cadette 11
Talbot Lago coach
Talbot Lago T26 coach
Talbot Lago T26 Grand Sport coupé
   Saoutchik
Talbot Lago T26 Record coupé
   Saoutchik
Talbot Lago T26 cabriolet Saoutchik
   ex–King Farouk

David Lillywhite, editor of England's highly respected *Octane* magazine, summarized the event succinctly: "The incredible cache of (mostly) thoroughbred cars on the grounds of a beautiful French chateau will surely go down in motoring history as one of the greatest-ever finds, including as it does a long-lost Ferrari SWB California Spyder, Maserati A6G Gran Sport, Hispano-Suiza H6, Bugatti Ventoux, Facel Vega Excellence, and many more. The news of this discovery quickly went viral."

Artcurial's sale was staged, with all of the cars displayed in one massive exhibition hall at the Paris Convention center as part of the annual Rétromobile Salon, which is perhaps the world's greatest car show. Each car artfully lighted to enhance the effect of its condition and also to minimize the visual impact of some of the more deteriorated examples.

The sale was, by any measure, a success, grossing $28.5 million. Top lots included, of course, the Ferrari California at a world record $18.5 million, with five cars selling at more than $1.1 million and ten cars selling for more than a half-million each.

What may be the icing on this rare and unusual cake is the display of all 59 Baillon Collection lots offered for sale in one giant convention hall salon. Some of the cars sat on their own wheels; others were either supported by special rigs or sat upon separate platforms. The brilliantly staged presentation and theater lighting was both striking and eerie.

Chapter 32

Scrapbook

BUT WAIT, THERE'S MORE!

As I noted in the introduction, I often came across cars, photos, and stories for which the information wasn't deep enough to warrant a separate chapter. Yet, in some cases, it was too cool to ignore or not include. So I've bundled them into this catchall chapter. Some of these cars are more "exotic" than others, but all are interesting and certainly represent ones I'd like to find abandoned in a barn.

1965 Austin-Healey 3000 Mk III

All photos courtesy of Auctions America.

This Healey showed up at a 2014 Auctions America sale in Auburn, Indiana, with precious little information available about its storage and history. It didn't matter because any legit "Big Healey" is a car of interest, and this one garnered plenty of looks, stares, and cell-phone camera photos.

The car appears to have been painted or perhaps fully restored at one time, before being stored for 23 years in a crowded, junk-filled garage or barn somewhere in the Midwest. The chalky, deteriorating paint was once a handsome glossy coat of authentic-looking British Racing Green.

This car will benefit from a complete and thorough restoration. However, it is nearly good enough to recommission mechanically, detail, and drive it without restoring. The body appears generally rust free, and the 3.0-liter straight-6 powertrain is present and complete. The interior seems to be well preserved even if it is terribly dusty. I'm betting that a new set of tires, new soft top, plus some serious soap and water action, will make this car a satisfying as-is driver.

Recall that the 3000 Mk III was the last generation of original Healeys; this beloved model went away after the 1967 model year. Someone else must have thought so as well, as it sold at auction for $11,660, which seems like a bargain to me, even though a show-quality restoration will be an expensive proposition.

Mid-1960s MGB

I spotted this not-so-bad chrome-bumpered MGB at a Cars N Coffee event in Virginia. I can't tell for sure if it's a real barn find or just a "creatively marketed" tired old sports car. Nobody seemed to know the car's owner or story, but it looked as it if could have been locked away in a barn or garage for some time. It was generally clean and appeared largely complete. Moreover, it presumably drove to and from this event under its own power, so if it had been stored, it had at least been returned to running condition. And the $5,000 asking price didn't seem half bad.

Of course, just staring at it gave me the barn finder's fantasy of buying the car on the spot, picking up a trunk-full of basic tools and the most obvious spare parts, and then driving it back to my Southern California home. Hey, the trip was only a couple thousand miles. I could pick up parts along the way, it would surely be much more romantic than my planned Coach-class flight home from Dulles to LAX.

Peugeot 204 Cabrio

Photo courtesy of Kirk Gerbracht.

I spotted this cute and compact Peugeot at a local car show. It appeared to be one of those cars needing little more than a mechanical recommissioning, paint job, and serious detailing to be a cheap and cheerful semi-collectible. Every piece of chrome and metal trim was present and in good shape. It was just waiting for some steel wool and chrome polish. The paint was faded and tired, but the body panels were excellent and rust free; the interior needed only a good scrubbing.

Some business cards were under the windshield wiper but no notes, price, or any other information about the car. My wife and a couple of my friends' wives were there at the same time, and each said she'd love to have it and be happy to cruise around town in it al fresco. The debate then began about which "nail polish paint color" it should be painted.

1967 Citroën DS21 Pallas

Photo courtesy of Kirk Gerbracht.

It's mathematically interesting that this book contains three separate and distinct Citroën barn finds.

This car attracted me for several reasons: I like Citroëns, and this Pallas model is among the highest premium trim levels for a DS21 at the time it was new.

This car offered two likely futures: It would make an excellent restoration candidate, because its coachwork and chassis appear complete and in solid condition. It would be an expensive restoration; it seemed a worthy piece to begin with if that were your goal. Alternatively, this could make an excellent parts car if your own DS needed major replacement components.

I particularly enjoyed the casual, matter-of-fact marketing approach outlined by the flyer taped to the door: "Red Fluid [the specification of mineral fluid used in the hydraulic system; some used corrosive "red" fluid, others used less corrosive "green" fluid]. Restoration Candidate. Late Mechanicals. Parts are everywhere. Includes replace-

ment decklid. Has a key. Motor turns freely. Estate sale: no paperwork. Will be sold with Bill of Sale. Paperwork may surface. Can deliver off this trailer. $3,000 or nearest offer. Let's haggle." Whimsical marketing, if nothing else.

Schlumpf Collection Bugattis

The story of the Swiss Schlumpf brothers and the world's largest and most private collection of Bugatti automobiles ever assembled has been told well and often. Some of the cars were pristine, some in unrestored "driver" condition, and others little more than piles of parts. Many were classic barn finds, some were stored prior to World War II and subsequently acquired by the Schlumpfs.

The Schlumpf brothers were in the textile business, and got themselves into some financial troubles with the French government. Ultimately, most of their assets were turned over to the French government. The result is a fabulous public museum in Mulhouse, France, called the National Automobile Association, Collection Schlumpf. Any serious, or even casual, automobile history enthusiast who finds himself or herself even remotely close to Alsace region in France must visit the museum.

American Peter Mullin is a man of substantial means and considerable taste, particularly for French and Art Deco–era art and automobiles. He has assembled an impressive collection and formed his own foundation and automotive museum in Oxnard, California. It's common for

museums to buy, sell, and trade assets among themselves to further their collections and exhibits. The Schlumpf museum has warehouses full of cars it'll likely never get around to restoring, and countless stores of parts.

A few years ago, Mullin acquired a small selection of original and unrestored cars to augment his own display of show-winning Bugattis and other French automobiles. It's a fascinating assemblage, some in true barn find condition, others appearing as original survivors best left unrestored, allowing their finishes and surfaces to be enjoyed as they are, and as a record of how they were originally engineered and built by the Bugatti factory in the 1920s and 1930s. Many of these cars are displayed, as found, in the Mullin Automotive Museum, as the Schlumpf Reserve Collection. As you can see from this photo, it's a very impressive lineup.

1966 Shelby GT350H

All photos courtesy of Kirk Gerbracht.

I was cruising my way through the Motor4Toys charity car show in Woodland Hills, California, in December 2014; I was stopped dead in my tracks by this multi-colored, extremely tatty-looking Mustang. Given its paint and stripe job, it appeared to be a 1966 Shelby GT350H Hertz "Rent A Racer" Mustang. Could it be? These are prized collectibles; nearly every one is tracked by its serial numbers and sought out by rabid Shelby fans. How could one of these great cars, in such a state of disassembly, just pop out of a yard, barn, or

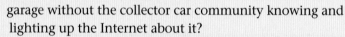

garage without the collector car community knowing and lighting up the Internet about it?

The car had a crowd around it as large as the gathering for any Ferrari, Jag, or Hemi in the show. The only information to be found was printed on a piece of paper taped to the trunk lid: "1966 Shelby 350 GT Hertz. This Shelby Mustang was just found in November 2014 sitting in East LA. It is a one owner car and approximately 1 of 50 sapphire blue with gold stripes. It was sitting for over 35 years in the original owner's back yard. It is complete with its original engine."

A walk around the car proved this to be so. The proper Shelby identification badge was riveted to the driver's side of the inner fenderwell under the engine compartment. Period-correct Rotunda tach mounted atop the dash. Automatic transmission. Gold GT350H stripes. Shelby goodies on the engine. The correct hoodscoop. Shelby badging.

Check, check, and check; all in place. Of course, all the Shelby bits could be faked onto a hacked-up 1966 Mustang fastback, but it and all of its patina looked kosher to my eyes. Subject to expert authentication and a concours-quality restoration, this car is worth hundreds of thousands of dollars. Let's hope it finds its way into the hands of a loving, wanting owner who'll invest the time and money to make it really right, then drive the wheels off it. What a find!

1964 Shelby Cobra 289

All photos courtesy of Kirk Gerbracht.

Shelby Cobra chassis CSX2435 was predicted to sell at Gooding & Company's January 2015 Scottsdale, Arizona, auction sale for $1 million to $1.4 million. It certainly had the right stuff, being a relatively late example of the small-block Cobra. It benefitted from all of the production updates that occurred along the way, including a 289-ci Ford V-8 instead of the earlier 260, as well as myriad chassis and frame improvements, including the all-important switch to rack-and-pinion steering.

This Cobra was scruffy-looking for sure, its black paint having suffered numerous scrapes and marginal-quality paint touch-ups along the way. However, it is the real-deal late-production small-block Cobra that everybody wants. Its life and history are documented in the all-important Shelby Registry. It was presented in original, unrestored condition; this Cobra had been in single-family ownership for 40 years.

Not everyone will love its tan-beige seats, but this Cobra absolutely had it all. If nothing else, it was a car that could be driven as is, sure to yield its share of positive and negative comments for its condition. Or it's the ideal candidate for a first-class platinum-level concours restoration. And it fell only a few bucks short of being a million-dollar baby, clearing Gooding's block that January day for $979,000 including buyer's commissions and fees. I assure you, it'll never sell for less than a million again.

1960 Aston Martin DB4 Series II

All photos courtesy of Kirk Gerbracht.

Two great DB4s in one book? Yes; actually three if you count David Sydorick's mouthwatering DB4GT Zagato. This one is gorgeous for sure, yet at the same time hurtin' for certain. It's a North American–spec car, left-hand drive from the factory, originally painted California Sage Green (some of which remains) over a beige leather interior. It was originally sold new in Alabama, then on to Texas in 1968. It has remained in the Texas family's ownership for approximately 45 years.

It is a well-equipped car, including factory chrome wire wheels, a Motorola model 319 radio, a 17-inch steering wheel, and a DB4 owner's kit. According to auction house Gooding & Company, the second owner was a pilot who used the car regularly from the time he acquired it in 1968 until he retired the car and stored it on his property until the early 1980s.

Gooding & Company presented the car at its January 2015 Scottsdale, Arizona, auction still wearing its Texas license plates. The paint has suffered innumerable scrapes, bangs, and questionable touch-up attempts, including either the replacement of the driver-side door, or its repainting in an entirely different color.

The car appears solid and sound, the ideal candidate for a platinum-level restoration, which is possible with this car, although it would certainly be expensive. There does not appear to be any notable rust or corrosion, indicating a structurally sound car ripe for the perfection spa treatment. Gooding's specialists estimated a $400,000 to 500,000 sale price and this proved to be spot-on. The car sold to a happy new owner for $462,000 including commissions and fees.

Porsche 356 Speedster

I spotted this faded early Porsche 356 Speedster at a Porsche club concours, not on the show grounds but out in the parking lot. The word around the event was that this car had been raced in its earlier days, laid up for mechanical reasons, and then parked in a garage for decades. The owner, whom I could not locate, did not respond to the note I left on the windshield requesting more information about the car. He (or she) is obviously proud of the car's somewhat forlorn "barn fresh" look and patina.

In spite of the semi-gutted interior and missing "Porsche" lettering on the nose, this car is in solid-looking condition, with no rust to be seen and little evidence of crash damage or poor repairs.

The early MobilGas Pegasus decal is a nice nostalgic touch, but I didn't see evidence of racing, racing number bubbles, or other decals. In terms of its past as a racer, it was hard to determine because there didn't appear to be any

mounting points, brackets, or holes where a roll bar, racing harnesses, or competition seatbelts might have been installed.

The car was a bit of a mystery; I'd never seen it before and have not since. It's a car that could be, and obviously was, driven in this as-found condition. Given its completeness and lack of apparent damage, it would be a superb restoration candidate. I hope I see it again some day.

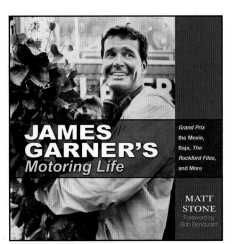
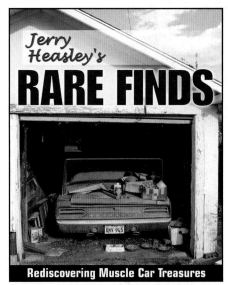
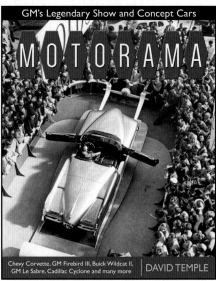
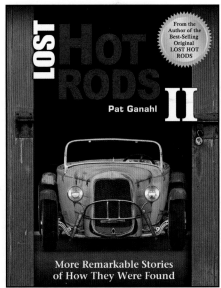